TENOR BANJO CHORDS FOR KIDS
... & BIG KIDS TOO!

by Nancy Eriksson & Tobe A. Richards

A Fretted Friends Beginners Publication for Cabot Books

Published by:
Cabot Books
Copyright © 2016 by Cabot Books
All rights reserved.

First Edition June 2016

ISBN-13: 978-1-906207-84-7

No part of this publication may be reproduced in any form or by any means without the prior consent of the publisher.

Cabot Books
3 Kenton Mews
Henleaze
Bristol
BS9 4LT
United Kingdom

Printed in The United States.

Visit our online site at www.frettedfriendsmusic.com
e-mail: cabotbooks@blueyonder.co.uk

CONTENTS

Introduction..4
Understanding the Chord Windows...5
All about Chords..6-11
Tenor Banjo Questions..12
Alternative Chord Names..13
Tenor Banjo Fingerboard Layout...14
Tuning Your Tenor Banjo..15
C Chords...16-22
C#/D♭ Chords...23-29
D Chords..30-36
D#/E♭ Chords...37-43
E Chords...44-50
F Chords...51-57
F#/G♭ Chords...58-64
G Chords..65-71
G#/A♭ Chords..72-78
A Chords..79-85
A#/B♭ Chords..86-92
B Chords..93-99
Moveable Chords..100-108

INTRODUCTION

Learning to play a musical instrument is a hobby that can last a lifetime. It can also lead to interesting career opportunities and into spheres such as teaching or part-time professional work.

Although some structured learning is needed by a beginner or intermediate student, the emphasis should still be to make music fun and not a daily chore to be endured rather than looked forward to. Young children in particular find it difficult to focus for long periods of time and if it feels too much like 'work', their interest will quickly fade. The days of sitting your bored 6-year-old in front of a piano and instructing them to practice their scales for the next hour are on the decline. For every child who benefits from this intense practice regime, another ten will be put off music altogether. On the flipside, if your child is engrossed in what he/she is doing, extended practice sessions are fine, within reason. But to generalise, 'less is more' within a learning environment, with plenty of encouragement thrown in to keep your child feeling positive regarding their progress.

The tenor banjo is a wonderful starter instrument for young children because of its relatively small size, closer fret spacing and moderate purchase price for a nice playable instrument. As your child progresses, you can always upgrade to a better model. Prices for a top quality banjo can often run into four figures, but you certainly shouldn't go down that road for a starter instrument.

Despite only having four strings, the tenor banjo is still capable of playing complex five, six or seven note chords. This is achieved by omitting the less important parts within the chord, but retaining the fundamental 'color' of the sound. Even the guitar makes similar compromises despite having two further courses of strings than the tenor banjo. To use a useful analogy, the eye doesn't need to see every inch of an elephant to know that it's an elephant. When it sees the trunk and the big ears, it knows what it is. Much the same reasoning is true regarding sound and harmony. The ear hears a thirteenth (a seven note chord), even if three of the notes are missing.

Good luck with your child's musical journey and remember music should always be fun!

UNDERSTANDING THE CHORD WINDOWS

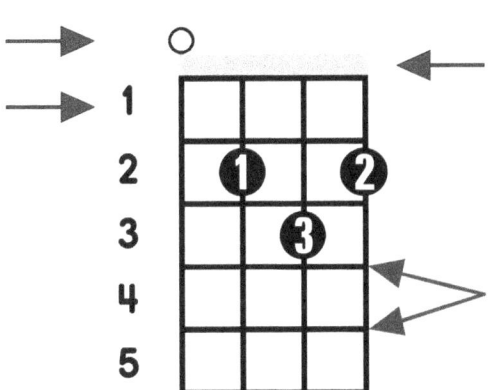

The circle at the top indicates an open string is to be played. You don't need to use any fingers on your left hand to play an open string.

Nut Position indicating the chord should be played within the span of the first five frets. Beyond that, the nut is omitted from the diagram.

The arrow pointing to the number column shows you which frets are used playing a particular chord shape.

The frets. No chord window in this or any other book will contain a chord that spans any more than five frets.

If you see an 'x' above a string in a chord window, it indicates the string shouldn't be played. Sometimes you might also see the 'x' directly on a string in the middle of a chord window. This tells you the string has to be damped using the pad on one your fingers directly above the string in question.

Most fingering positions will be dictated by where the notes are situated on the fingerboard. Others will be down to personal preference.

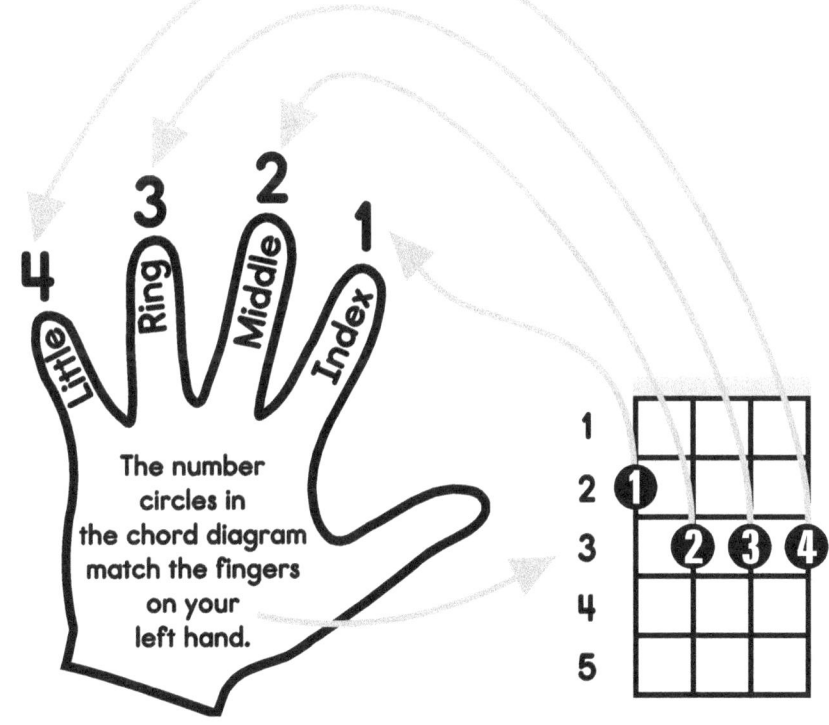

The number circles in the chord diagram match the fingers on your left hand.

ALL ABOUT CHORDS

Q: Does my young child need to learn chord theory?
A: Music is only enjoyable for young children if it's fun! So my advice would be to prioritise the 'hands on' approach and leave the more complex whys and hows until they're going to be receptive towards them. My one proviso being that they learn to use the chord window diagrams on their own. This also encourages the child to explore and achieve new sounds without the constant guidance of having an adult present.

Q: Should we skip this section of the book then?
A: Not necessarily. It may help if you can add some input yourself while your child is learning to play. The information is also accessible for older children and young adults.

Q: For how long should my child practice?
A: A young child shouldn't be playing for more than 30 minutes at a time unless they really want to. When playing becomes a chore, their interest is likely to wane. Physically, it can also be quite taxing on little fingers especially with the tenor banjo's metal strings.

Q: What should I look for when buying a tenor banjo?
A: The criteria should be playability first and foremost. Check every fret on every string to make sure you don't get any buzz from them. Also pay careful attention to the 'action' (the height of the strings above the fingerboard/fretboard. If it takes a lot of pressing down, your child won't be able to properly play chords higher up the neck. It will also affect the intonation of the banjo, making some chords sound out of tune. You don't have to spend a fortune to get a good starter instrument.

Q: What if he or she breaks a string?
A: Always keep a spare set in a drawer, as this is quite likely to happen from time to time. There are countless videos on YouTube and other sources showing how to put on a new string.

Q: How should I or my child tune the tenor banjo?

A: There are a variety of different ways to do this. Option 1: tune to a piano or electronic keyboard. This will pretty much ensure that you have the correct tuning. Option 2: use a chromatic tuner. These don't have to be particularly expensive, but you will have to replace batteries occasionally. Option 3: buy a set of pitch pipes designed for the tenor banjo. Not quite as accurate as the first two options, but a nice low tech solution for a child to blow and more fun than the other two.

Q: What is a chord?

A: It's a collection of three or more notes played at the same time.

Q: Are there any chords which break the rules on chord construction?

A: Yes. The 5th chord (C5, G5 etc.). Technically, this isn't a true chord as it only contains 2 intervals, a root and a fifth. But for the sake of convenience, it's allowed to gate crash the party and join the rest of it's musical cousins.

Q: What are intervals?

A: Intervals are the separate notes that make up a chord. The musical distance between each note tells you what type of chord it is. For example the chord of C major is a three note chord. It contains the notes C, E and G. The C is the first or 'root' note, the E is the 3rd note and the G is the 5th note (known as the 'Perfect Fifth'). To understand this better, try counting up the white notes from the 'C' on a piano keyboard.

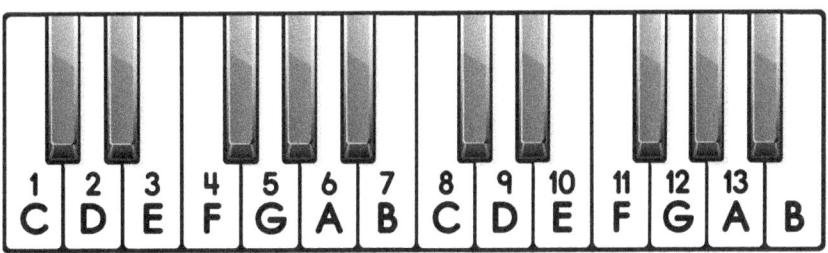

Q: What is a triad?
A: A chord with three different notes in it. Examples include G (major), Bm (minor), D+ (augmented) and Asus4 (suspended fourth).

Q: What is a seventh?
A: It's an extra interval added to the end of a triad. There are many types of 7th chord, but the ones you'll use the most are the 'dominant' 7th and the 'major' 7th. Using the key of C as an example they will mainly be written as C7 (dominant) and Cmaj7 (major seventh).

Q: Which numbers aren't used in the naming of chords?
A: An 8th, a 10th and a 12th. All the others are used (1st or root, 2nd, 3rd, 4th, 5th, 6th, 7th, 9th, 11th and 13th. Some notes are also shared. The 2nd is the same note as a 9th, a 4th shares with the 11th and the 6th with the 13th. You can see this in action on the previous page.

Q: What is a chromatic scale?
A: It's a scale that includes all twelve notes featured in popular music. This includes all the white notes (the naturals) and black notes (sharps and flats) found a piano keyboard. Every chord in this book or any other piece of music includes a combination of some of these notes. The example below features the scale of C major.

Root | Minor | Major | Minor | Major | Perfect | Augmented or Diminished | Perfect | Minor | Major | Minor | Major
or 1st | 2nd | 2nd | 3rd | 3rd | 4th | 4th | 5th | 5th | 6th | 6th | 7th | 7th

Q: What is a ninth?
A: A ninth is a five note chord, consisting of a triad with the addition of a seventh and a ninth note. Again, it's most widely used types are the dominant ninth (for example, F9 or A9), the minor ninth (Dm9 or Fm9) and the major ninth (Dmaj9 or Bmaj9). In some instances the root, 3rd or 5th notes are omitted, depending on the chord. This doesn't greatly affect the overall sound, though.

Q: What is an extension?

A: A chord which goes beyond the scope of triads and sevenths. Basically, extensions are additional notes placed above the triad or seventh in a musical stave (or in piano terms, higher up the keyboard). These include 9ths, 11ths and 13ths in all their different incarnations. It's important to understand these are, for theoretical purposes, always placed above the seventh. Or in layman's terms higher up the scale. The confusion comes when you start to realise a 9th is identical to a 2nd (in the scale of C, a 'D' note).

Q: So why is the ninth note the same as the second note?

A: This takes a little grasping, but if you remember that if your note goes higher than the 7th, it's a ninth, but if it's lower, it'll be a 2nd. An example of this would be Csus2, which contains the root note of C, a 2nd or suspended D note and a G (the perfect fifth).

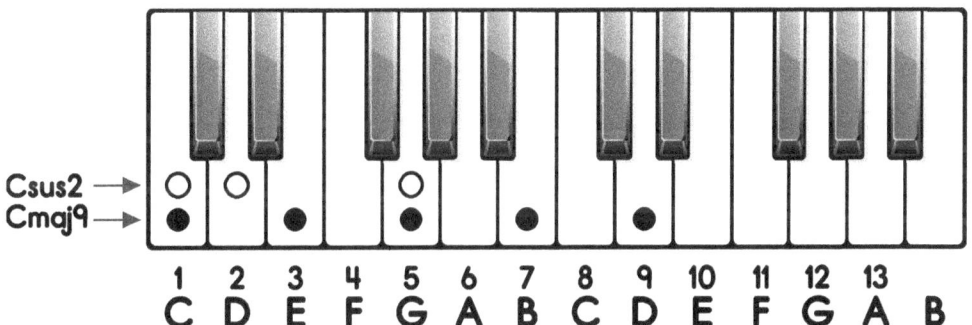

Q: So do other extensions share a note?

A: Yes. Other examples include the 11th (which is also a 4th) and the 13th (which shares a note with the 6th).

Q: Do elevenths and thirteenths have any particular properties?

A: Yes. In most cases the 3rd is omitted from eleventh chords and in turn, the 11th from the majority of thirteenths as they're deemed unnecessary and arguably create unwanted dissonance. In other instances the chords can be further truncated without changing the overall integrity of the sound.

Q: What is a suspended chord?

A: It's simpler to think of suspended chords as a stepping stone to a major or resolving chord. In effect the third has been left in a state of suspension by either raising it to a fourth (sus4) or lowering it to a second (sus2). Sevenths also provide versions of the suspended chord in the form of C7sus4 or E7sus2 (just to give two examples).

Q: What is a diminished chord?

A: A diminished chord has a dissonant quality to it where the third and fifth notes in a triad are flattened by a semi-tone. Again, using C as an example, C major (C-E-G) is altered to C° (C-E♭-G♭). A second version of a diminished chord is also used in many forms of music, the diminished seventh (e.g. C°7). This retains the elements of a standard diminished chord, adding a double flat in the seventh (C-E♭-G♭-B♭♭). A B♭♭ in this case is to all intents and purposes really an A note.

Q: What is an augmented chord?

A: An augmented chord basically performs the opposite task to a diminished one. Instead of lowering the fifth by a semi-tone, it raises it by the same interval. A C+ (augmented) chord contains the triad of C-E-G♯. The major root and third are retained and the fifth is sharpened.

Q: What is a sixth chord?

A: A sixth (or major sixth) is a major or minor triad with an added major sixth note. In the case of C6, it features the notes C-E-G-A. A sixth can also be minor, adding a gloomy quality to the chord. The only difference with the previous example is that the 3rd note is flattened. The resultant intervals would be C-E♭-G-A in the case of Cm6.

Q: What is a minor chord?

A: A minor chord, just like its major sibling is a triad. It always features the same root and fifth notes as a major chord, but takes on a more dramatic flavor by lowering or flattening the 3rd by a semi-tone. Cm includes the intervals of C-E♭-G (compared to C major, C-E-G). The other really important type of minor chord is the minor seventh. This is like a combination of the dominant seventh and the standard minor triad melded together. Both the 3rd and the 7th are flattened.

A typical minor seventh chord would be written Cm7, F#m7 or Am7, just to give three different examples.

Q: What is an added chord?

A: It's a note or notes that are added to a basic chord to create a generally fuller sound. A prime example of this would be the added ninth chord. Here, the basic triad is supplemented by the addition of a ninth. So again, going back to C major (C-E-G), when you add the ninth, it becomes Cadd9 (expressed in intervals as C-D-E-G). This chord can also be written as Cadd2, depending on whether it's viewed by the composer as a major second (Cadd2) or a ninth (Cadd9). Either way, it's the same chord. Other popular added chords include a minor version of the triad with an added interval (Cmadd9 or Cmadd2). This is a basic minor chord with the major second or ninth added (C-D-E♭-G in the case Cmadd9 or Cadd2).

Q: What are inversions?

A: In the root version of a chord, the notes run in their correct order from lowest to highest. In the case of G major, it would be G-B-D. With an inversion of the same chord, the notes would run in a different order. For example, the 1st inversion of G major would be B-D-G and the 2nd, D-G-B. In general, triads sound more or less the same when they're inverted. This becomes less true though, as the chords become more complex. Take a Cmaj7 (major seventh) chord in it's root position (C-E-G-B). It has a gentle relaxed feeling to it. Then move it up to the 1st inversion and it suddenly takes on a slightly unpleasant dissonant quality. Another interesting example of a clear sonic difference between the root note and one of its inversions is C6 (C-E-G-A). When you move up to its 3rd inversion, you're basically playing the chord of Am7, which sounds quite different from a major sixth chord.

Q: Some chords are called by different names in different music books. What should we do?

A: The alternative chord names reference chart on page 13 should sort out the confusion. The examples are in the key of C, but equally apply to all twelve keys.

TENOR BANJO QUESTIONS

Q: **How is the tenor banjo tuned and strung?**

A: Standard tuning for the tenor banjo is CGDA (low to high). This is also referred to as 'jazz' tuning and the subject of this book. The main alternative to this is the lower pitched 'Irish' tuning (GDAE) which is favored by folk music players. Both are tuned in fifths, with the Irish version pitched a fourth lower than standard tuning. One important thing to know when buying strings for the tenor banjo is to make sure you select the correct gauge. Because of the lower pitch, Irish tuning requires a heavier set of strings.

Q: **How many members of the banjo family are there?**

A: The banjo family is quite extensive, with the most popular members being the tenor banjo, the 5-string bluegrass (or 'G' banjo), the plectrum banjo, the banjolele (or banjo-ukulele) and the 6-string guitar banjo. The latter two are to all intents and purposes 'banjo-ized' ukuleles and guitars. Other less common instruments also exist including the electric 5-string banjo, the mandolin banjo (tuned like a mandolin with 8 strings), the Seeger banjo (a long scale 5-string) and the bass banjo (tuned EADG like a bass guitar or double bass). There are other variants, but these are the main ones.

Q: **How many frets does a tenor banjo have?**

A: The tenor banjo generally features either 17 frets for a short scale model (20-21.5") or 19 frets for a regular long scale (22-23"). The shorter scale will be a little easier to play for younger children, but equally the longer scaled instrument won't be beyond most small hands.

Q: **What type of tenor banjo should we buy?**

A: There are two basic types to choose from - the open-back or the resonator. There are pros and cons to each, but arguably the open-back is a better choice for a younger child as the resonator is a lot heavier to hold. The resonator is also considerably louder as the name suggests. Both can be played on a lap or standing up supported by a strap. If you have noise issues, the open-back is probably a more sensible option, as the resonator is designed to be heard clearly within the context of a band or group. The other thing to consider is occasionally you'll need to replace the banjo head and bridge. To do this there are many very good 'how to' videos on the internet. It is a bit of a fuss, but needs to be done when the head starts getting slack and loses its tone.

ALTERNATIVE CHORD NAMES

C	**CM** or **Cmaj**	M	**major**
Cm	**Cmin** or **C-**	m	**minor**
C-5	**C♭5** or **C(♭5)**	-	**minor**
C°	**Cdim**	dim	**diminished**
C5	**C Power Chord** or **C(no 3rd)**	°	**diminished**
Csus2	**C(sus2)** or **C2**	sus	**suspended**
Csus4	**Csus** or **C(sus4)**	aug	**augmented**
C+	**Caug, C+5** or **C(#5)**	+	**augmented**
C6	**CM6** or **CMaj6**	add	**added**
Cadd9	**Cadd2**	dom	**dominant**
Cm6	**C-6** or **Cmin6**	△	**delta / major seventh**
Cmadd9	**Cmadd2** or **C-(add9)**	#	**sharp**
C°7	**Cdim7**	x	**double sharp**
C7	**Cdom**	♭	**flat**
C7sus4	**C7sus, C7(sus4)** or **Csus11**	♭♭	**double flat**
C7-5	**C7♭5**		
C7+5	**C7+** or **C7#5**		
C7-9	**C7♭9** or **C7(add♭9)**		
C7+9	**C7#9** or **C7(add#9)**		
Cm7	**C-7, Cmi7** or **Cmin7**		
Cm7-5	**Cm7♭5** or **C-7-5**		
Cm(maj7)	**Cm#7, CM7-5, CmM7** or **C-△**		
Cmaj7	**CM7** or **C△(Delta)**		
C9	**C7(add9)**		
Cm9	**C-9** or **Cmin9**		
Cmaj9	**CM9, Cmaj7(add9), C△9** or **CM7(add9)**		
C11	**C7(add11)**		
C13	**C7/6(no 9th)** or **C7(add13)**		

The majority of music books will use the chords featured in the first column (on the far left), but should you come across alternatives, consult this guide for other naming conventions. The list on the right includes most of the symbols and abbreviations that you're likely to encounter in the majority of music books.

THE TENOR BANJO FINGERBOARD LAYOUT

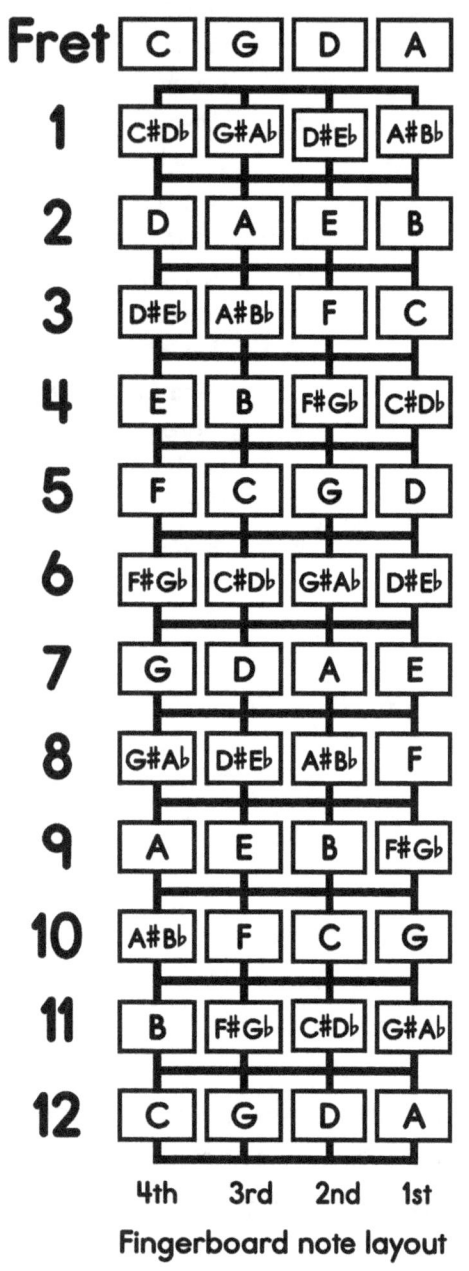

Fingerboard note layout

The four notes across the top of the left-hand diagram represent the four open strings of a tenor banjo. If you stood the banjo up on its bottom side facing you, the notes on the fingerboard would be identical to the diagram on the left.

When you reach the 12th fret the pattern repeats, again starting with CGDA. This is where the new octave starts on each string. An octave is a series of eight consecutive notes ending on the root note you started with. In the key of C, the intervals are C, D, E, F, G, A, B and C (all white notes). A complete octave will also include the semi-tones (a further five black notes). In other keys, it'll be a mixture of naturals, sharps and flats.

Tenor Banjo CGDA tuning in standard notation

TUNING YOUR TENOR BANJO

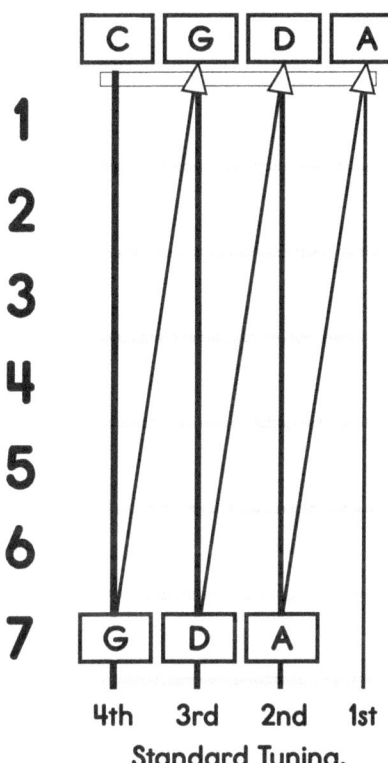

Standard Tuning.

Tuning the tenor banjo by fretting at different intervals on the fingerboard.

If you're playing with other people, it's important that your tenor banjo is tuned accurately. With standard tuning, always tune the 4th 'C' string first and follow the arrows shown in the lefthand diagram, tuning from left to right. If you're practicing on your own, it's less important to tune to true concert pitch as long as all the strings are in tune with each other.

The tenor banjo is tuned in fifths, so if you remember that the 7th fret is always exactly a fifth higher than the open string, tuning becomes a fairly straightforward process.

To tune your tenor banjo properly, it's best to use an electronic chromatic tuner, but if there isn't one available, you can tune it to a guitar, piano/electronic keyboard or pitch pipes. The following tuning grid gives the correct fingering positions on the guitar fingerboard and piano keyboard.

Tenor Banjo	Guitar	Piano
1st string (A)	1st string (E) fretted at the 5th fret	1st A above middle C
2nd string (D)	2nd string (B) fretted at the 3rd fret	1st D above middle C
3rd string (G)	3rd open string (G)	1st G below middle C
4th string (C)	5th string (A) fretted at the 3rd fret	1st C below middle C

C Chords

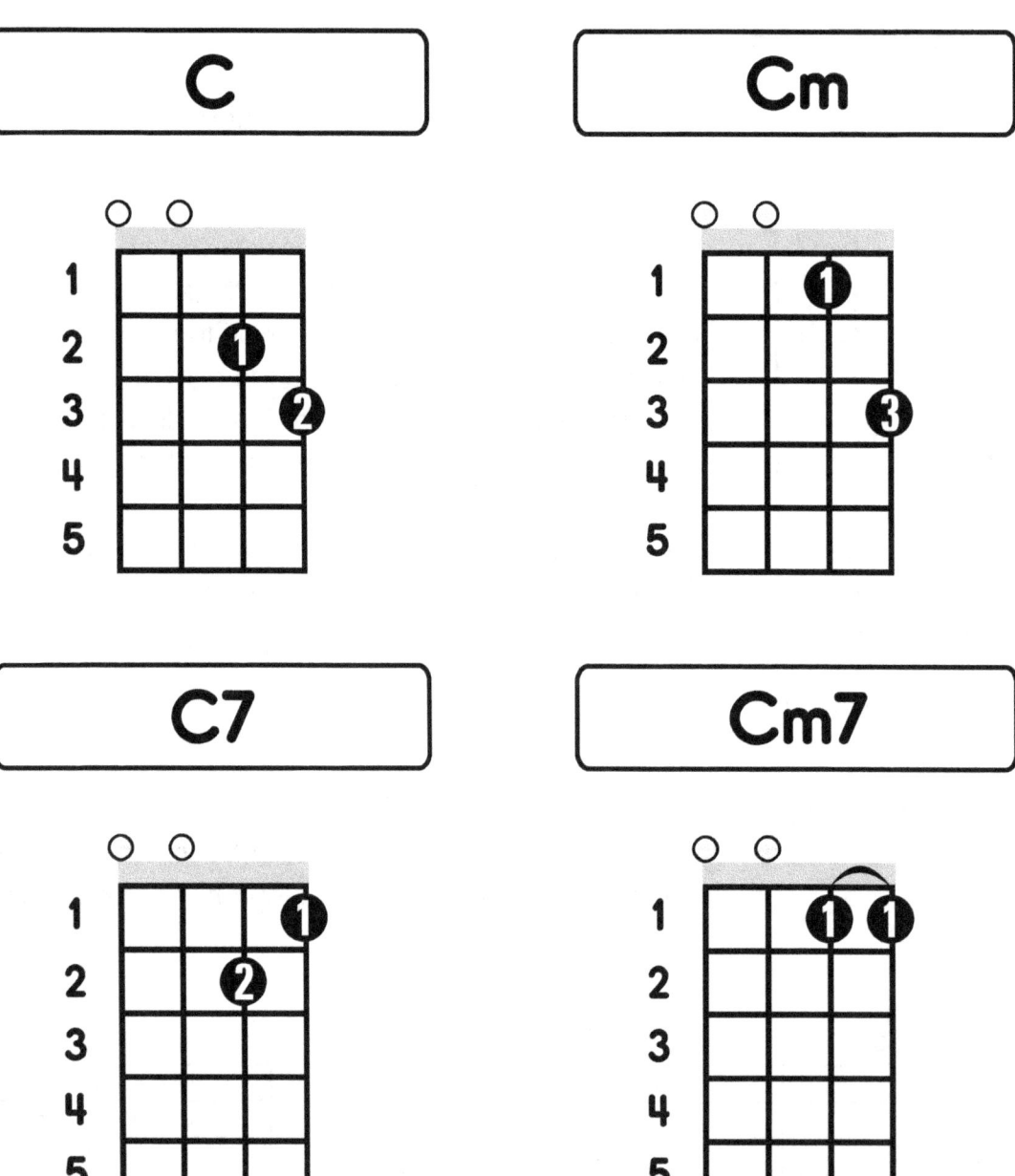

C Chords

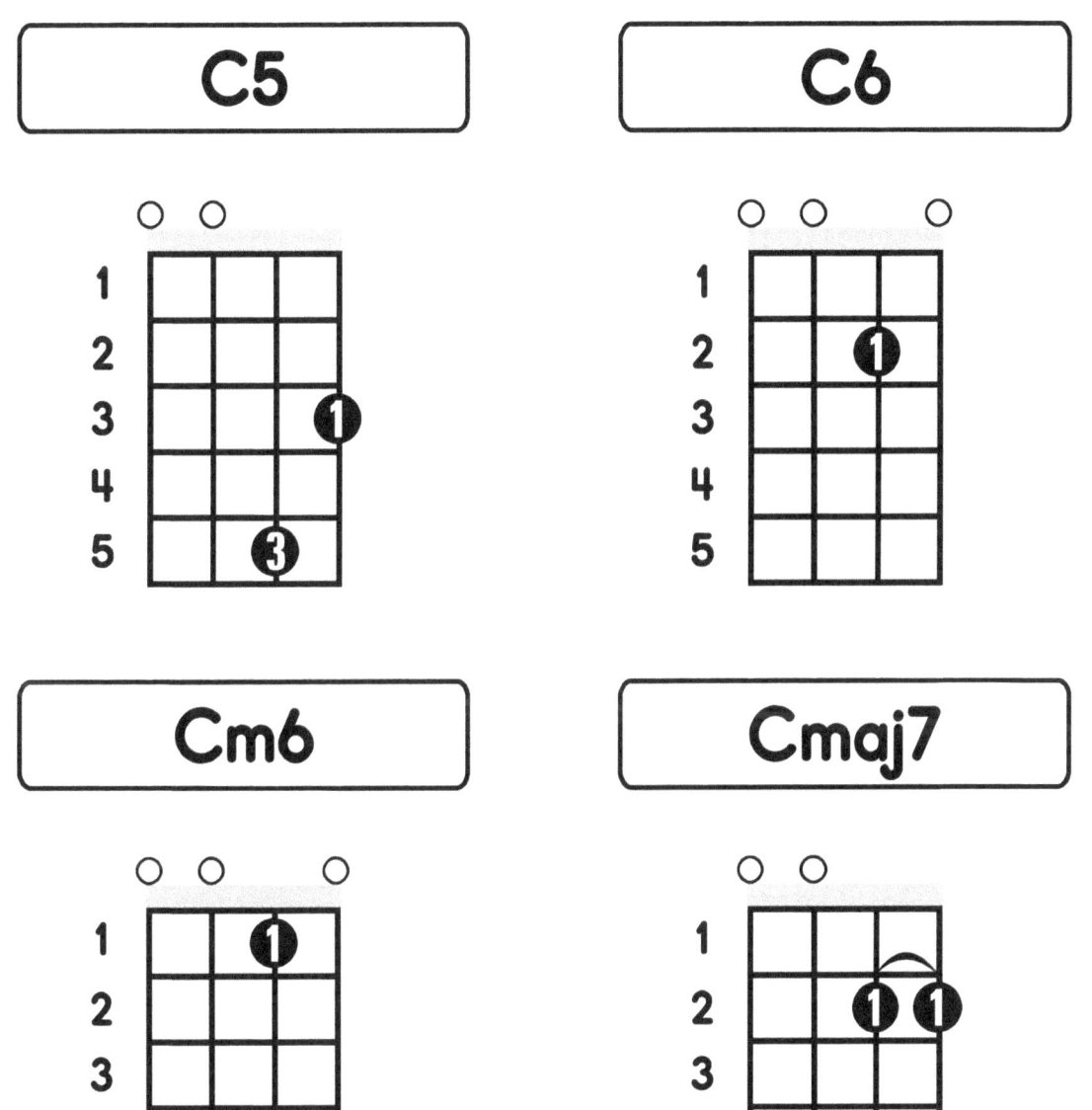

C Chords

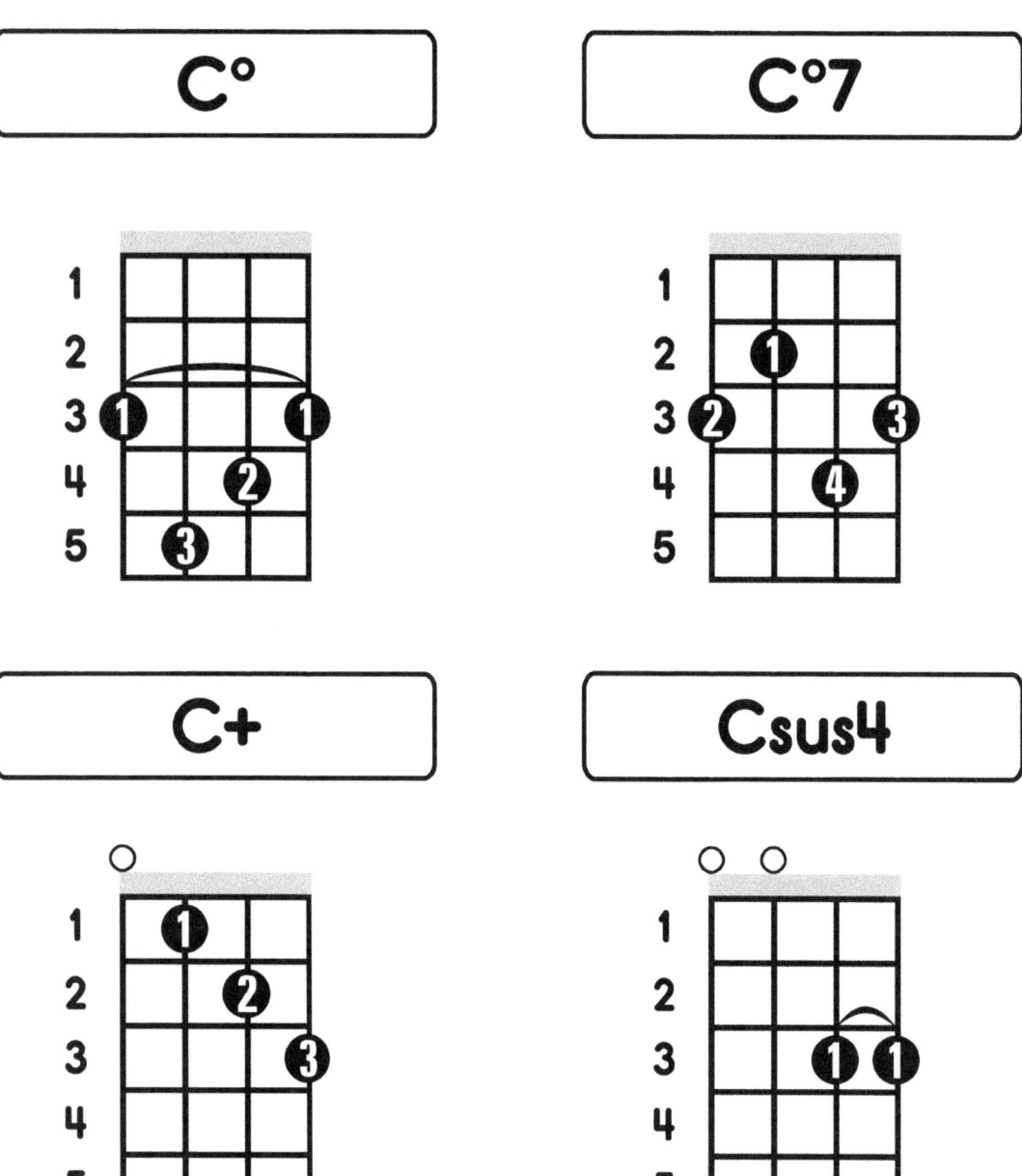

C Chords

Cadd9
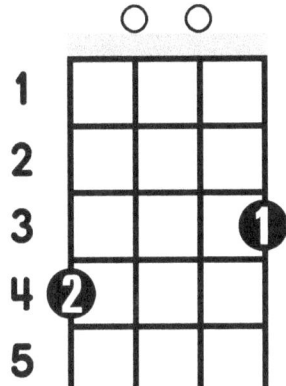

Cmadd9
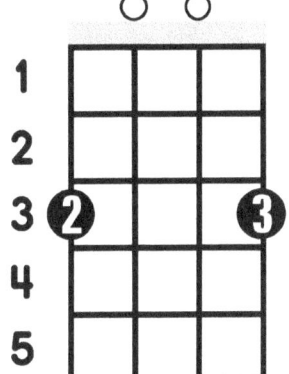

Cm7-5
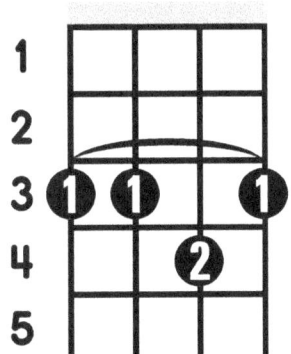

C7sus4
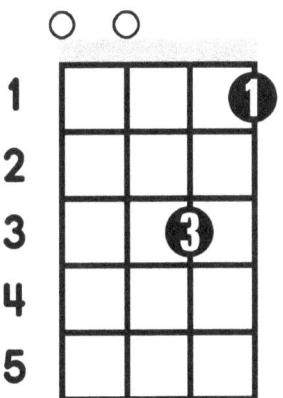

C Chords

Csus2
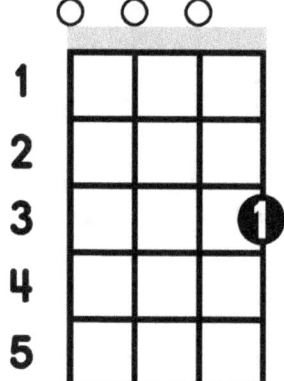

Cm(maj7)
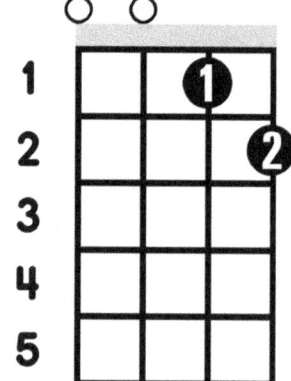

C7-5
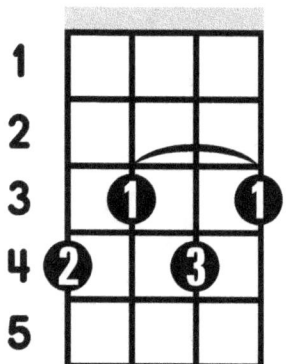

C7+5
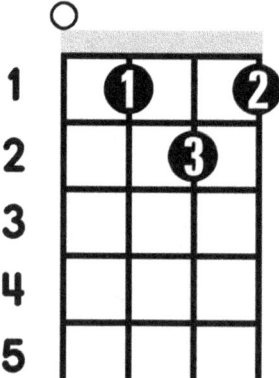

C Chords

C7-9
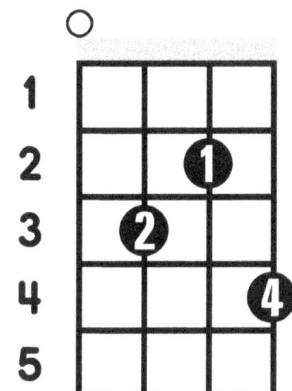

C7+9
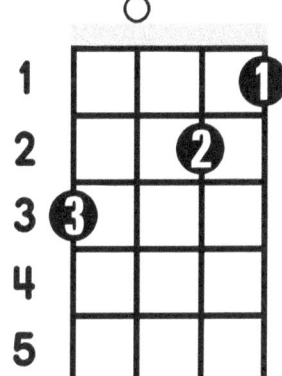

C-5
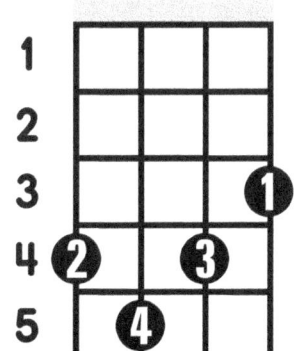

C9
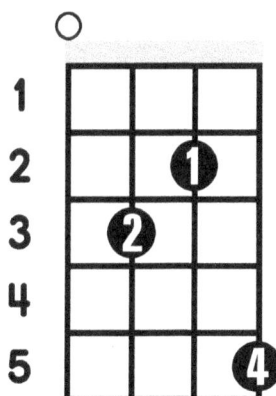

C Chords

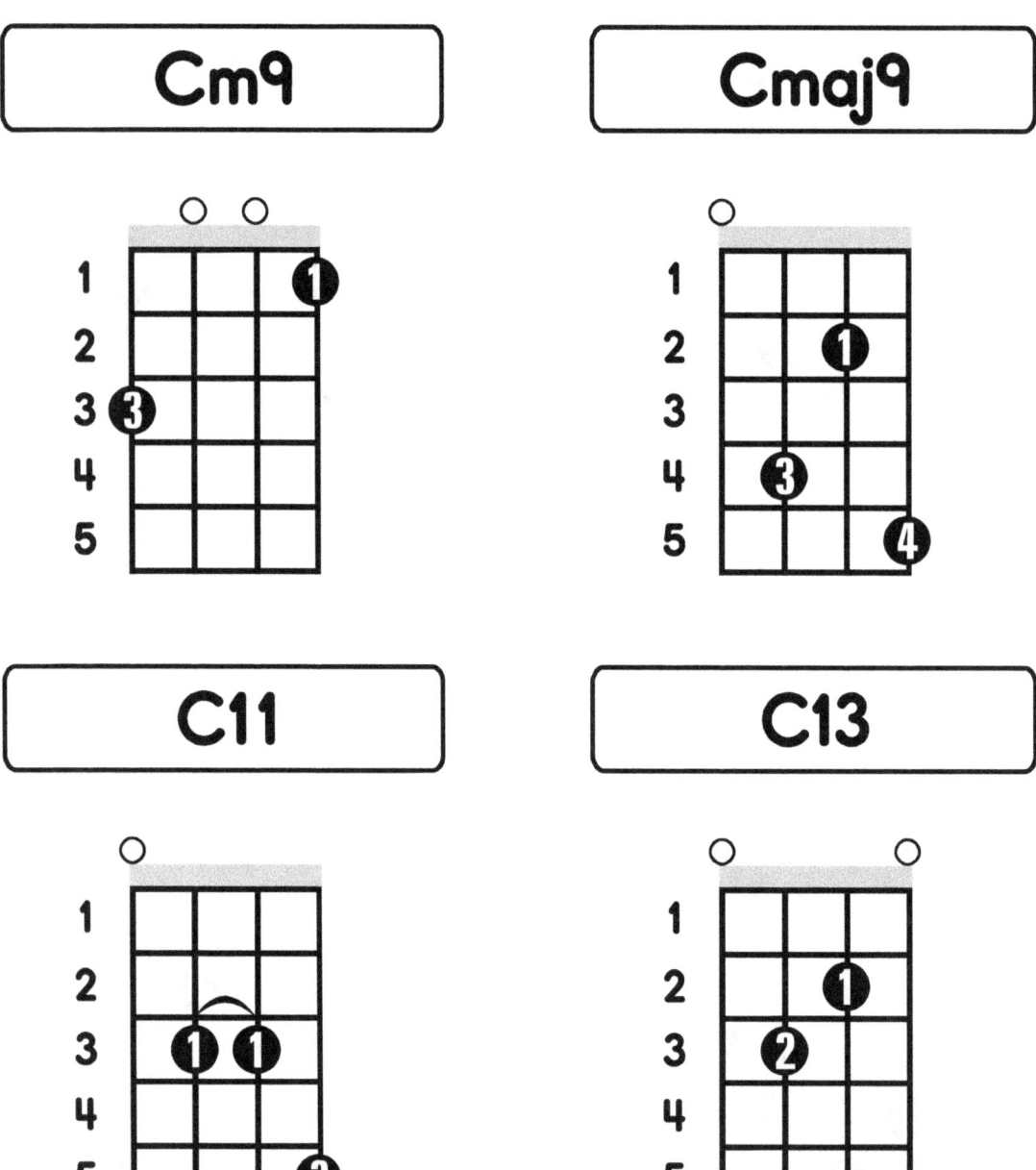

C# / D♭ Chords

D♭

D♭m

D♭7

D♭m7

C# / D♭ Chords

D♭5
D♭6
D♭m6
D♭maj7

C# / D♭ Chords

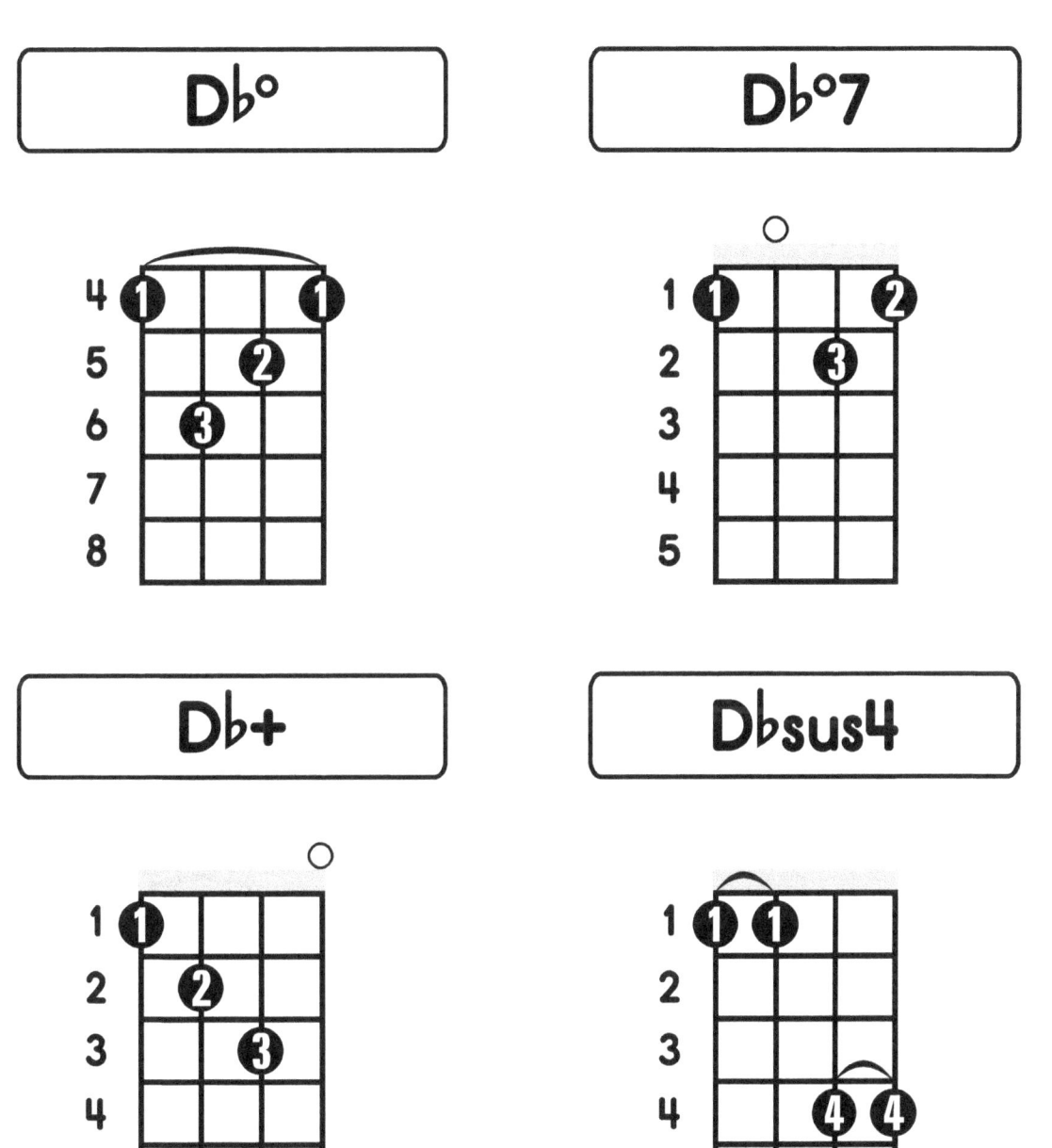

C# / D♭ Chords

D♭add9
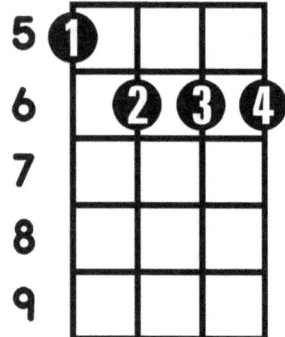

D♭madd9
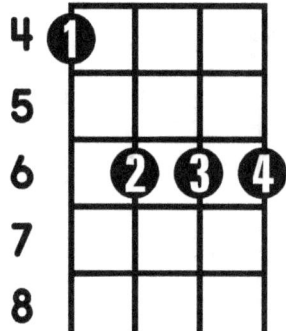

D♭m7-5
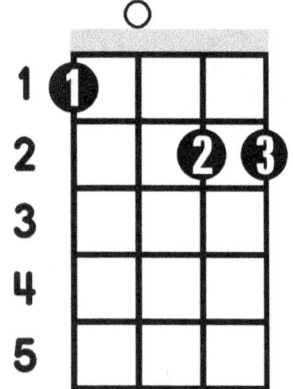

D♭7sus4
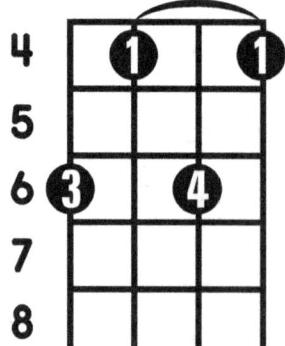

C# / D♭ Chords

D♭sus2

D♭m(maj7)

D♭7-5

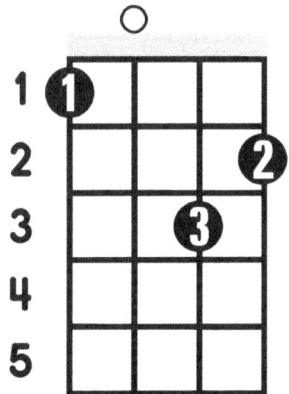

D♭7+5

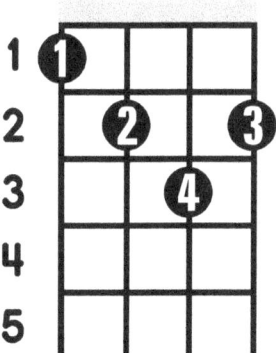

C# / D♭ Chords

D♭7-9
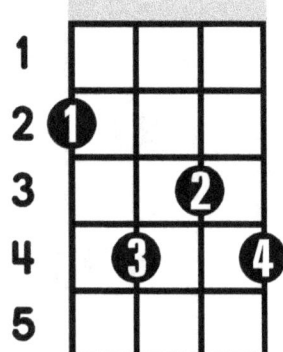

D♭7+9
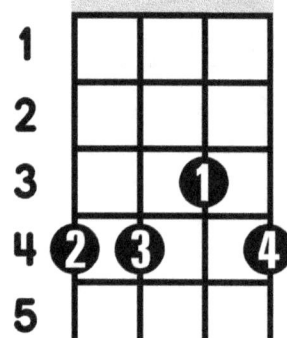

D♭-5
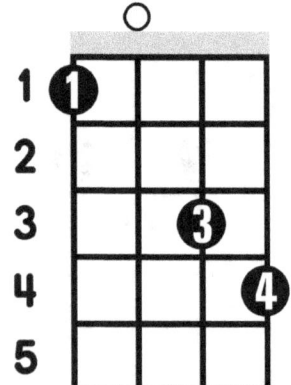

D♭9
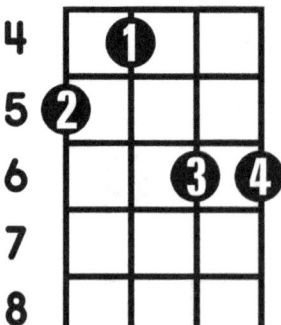

C# / D♭ Chords

D♭m9
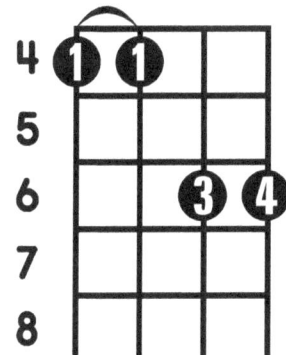

D♭maj9
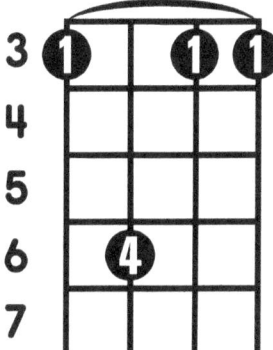

D♭11
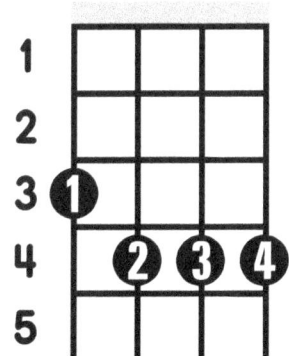

D♭13
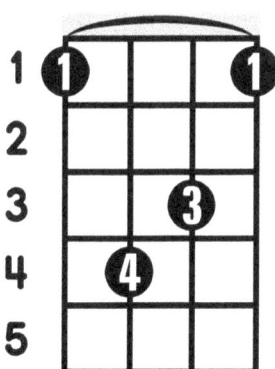

D Chords

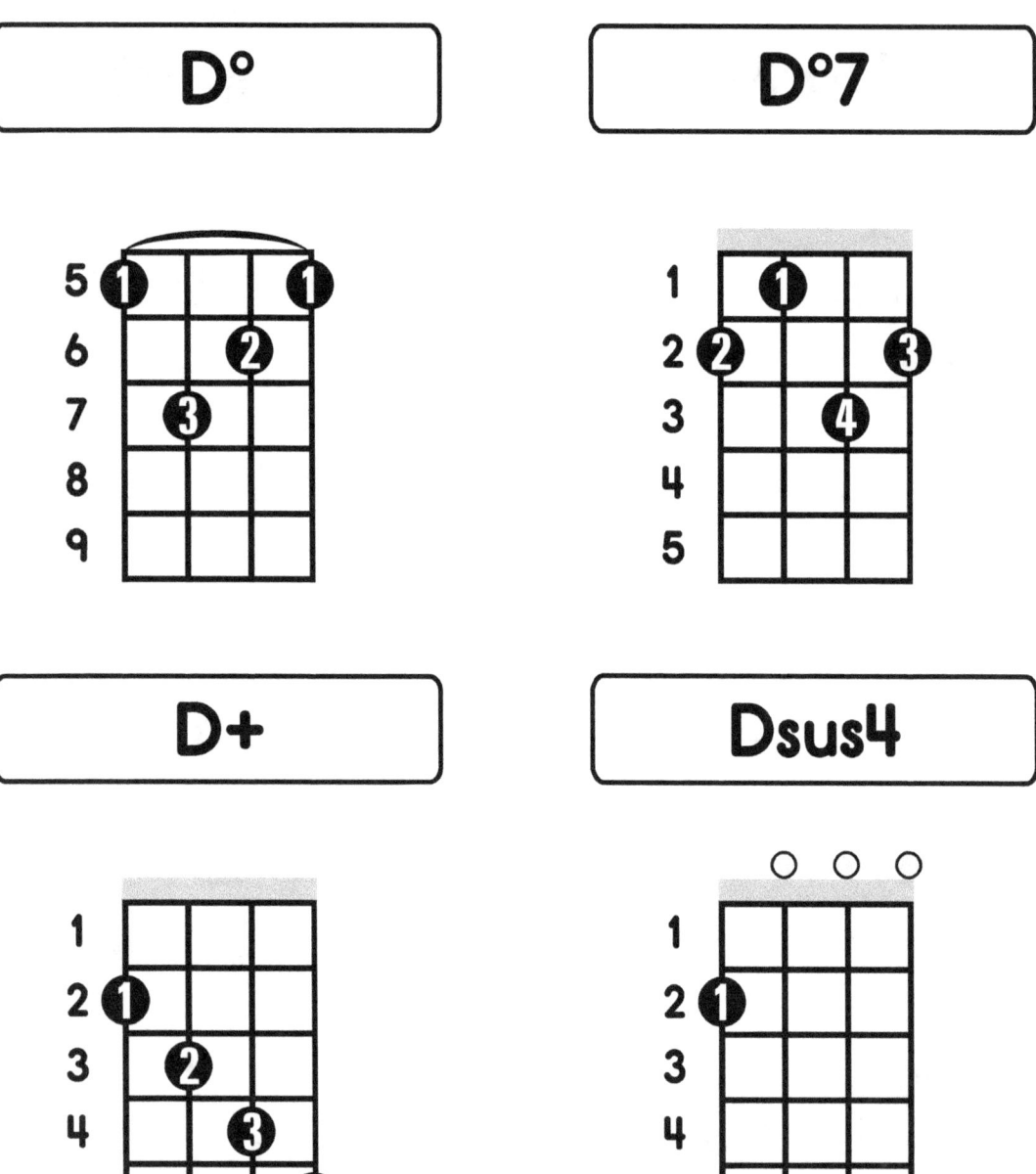

D Chords

D5

D6

Dm6

Dmaj7

D Chords

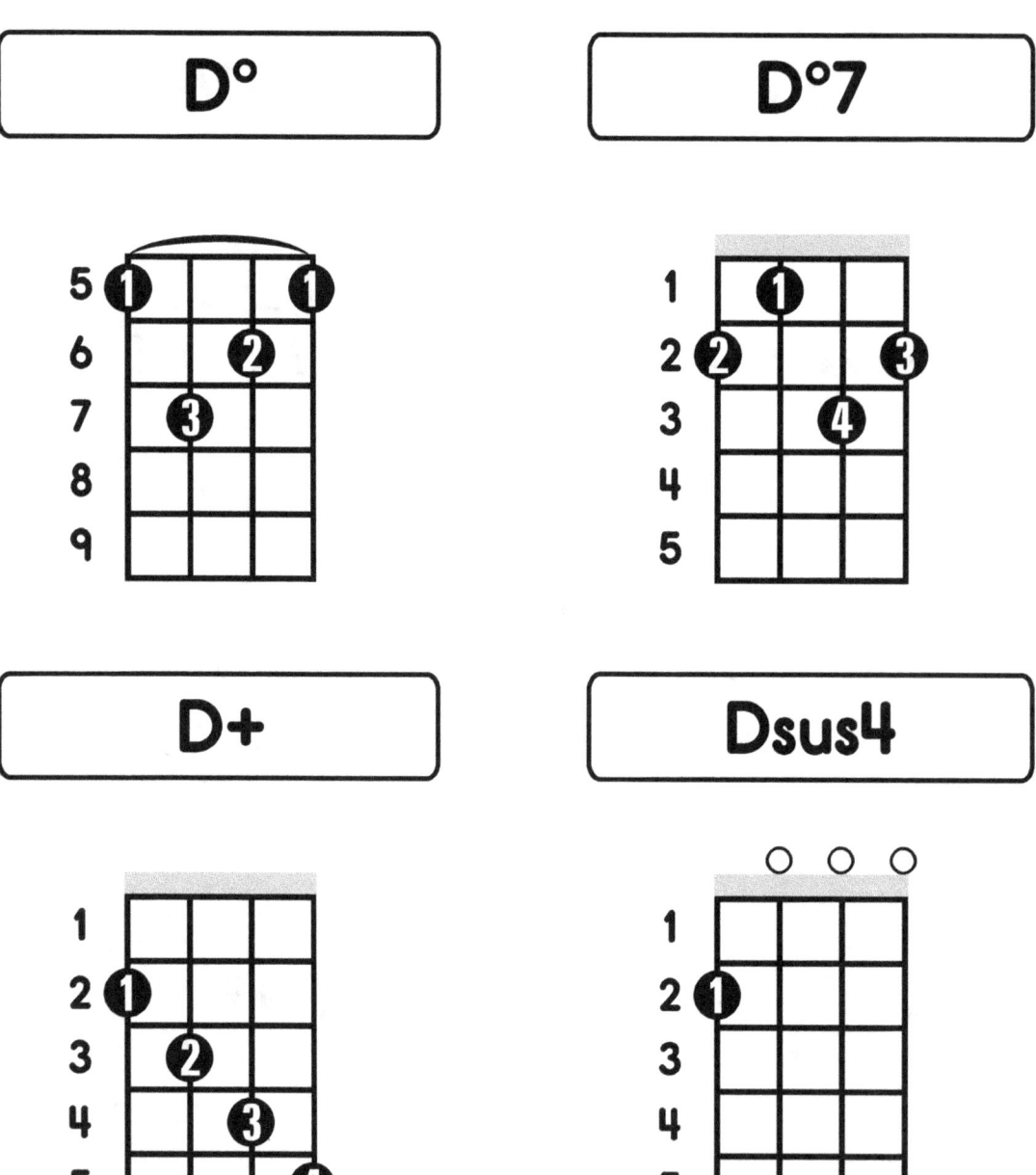

D Chords

Dadd9
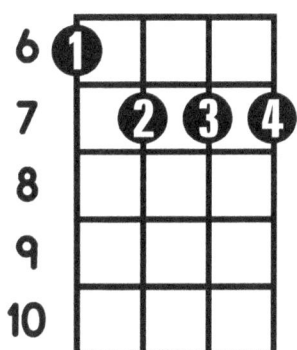

Dmadd9
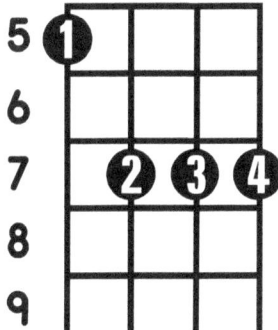

Dm7-5
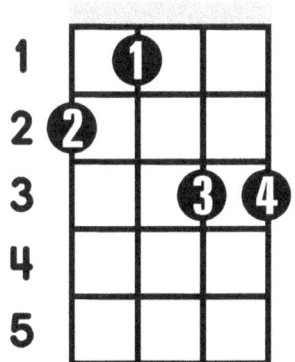

D7sus4
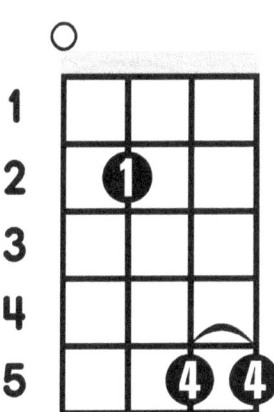

D Chords

Dsus2
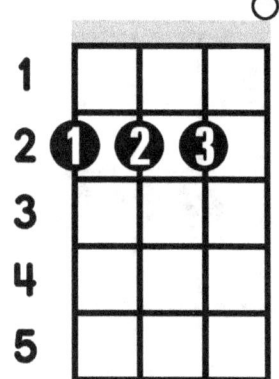

Dm(maj7)
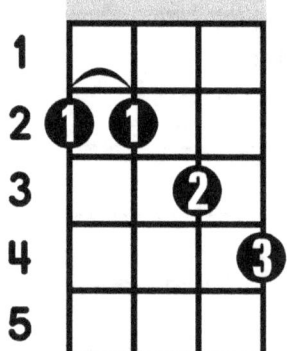

D7-5
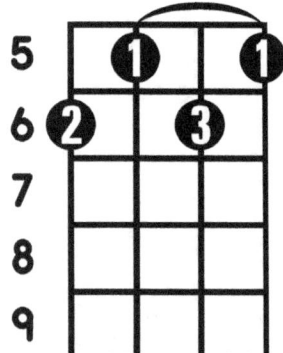

D7+5
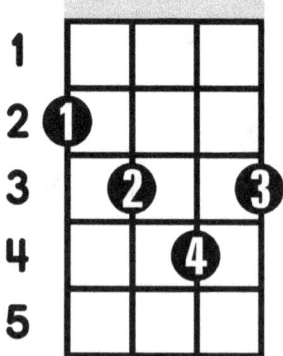

D Chords

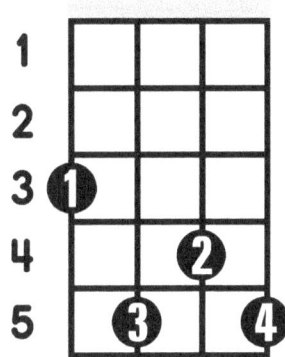

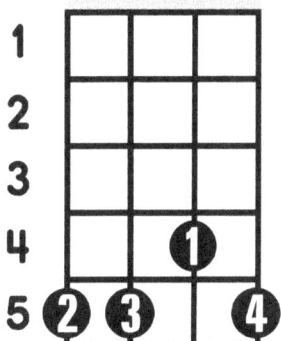

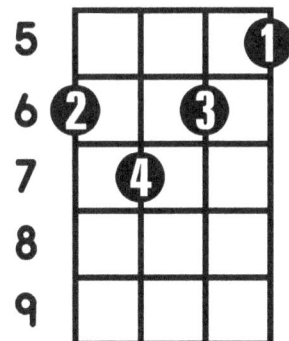

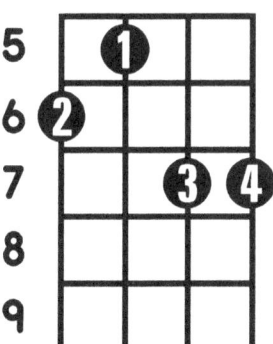

D Chords

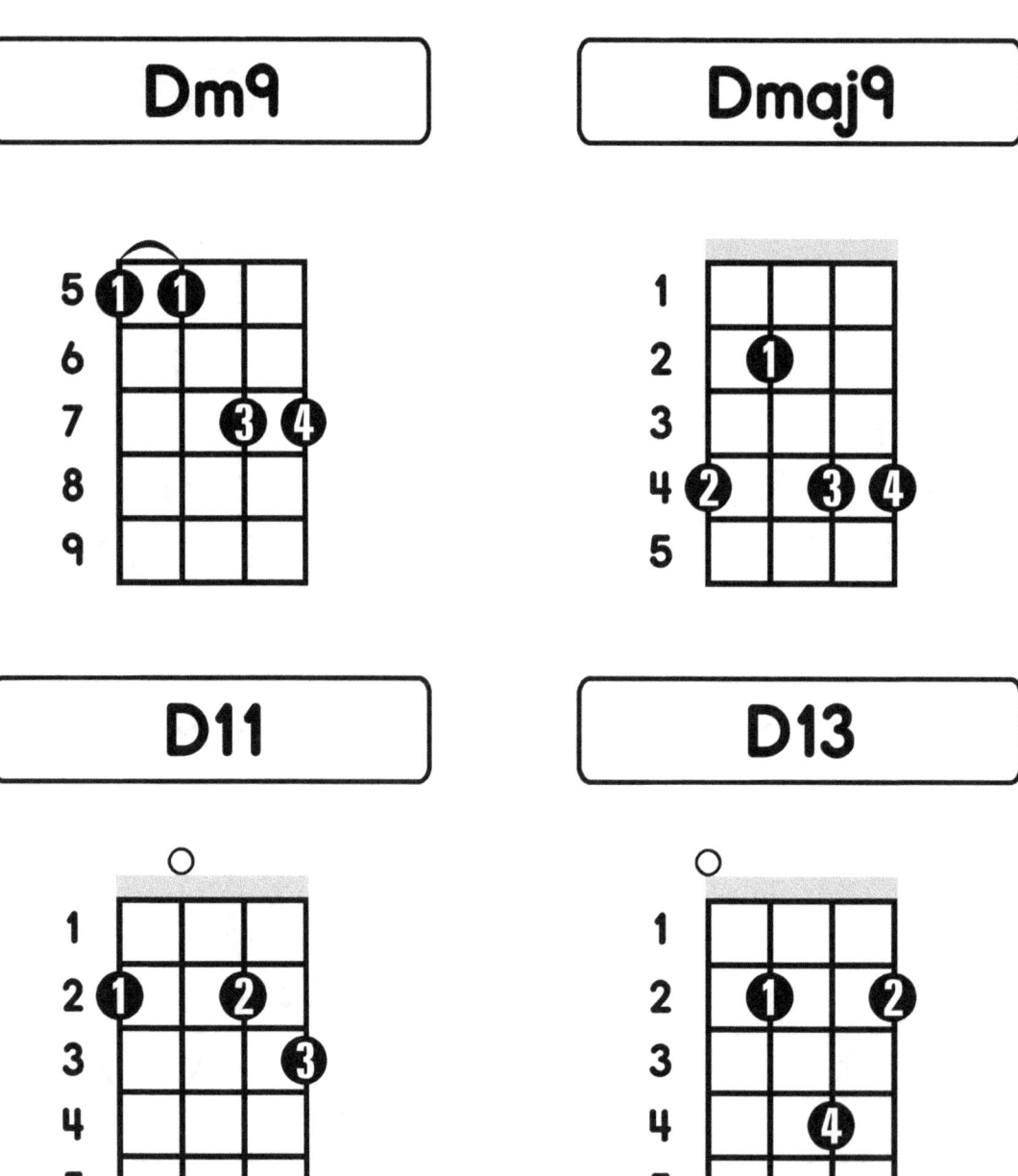

D♯ / E♭ Chords

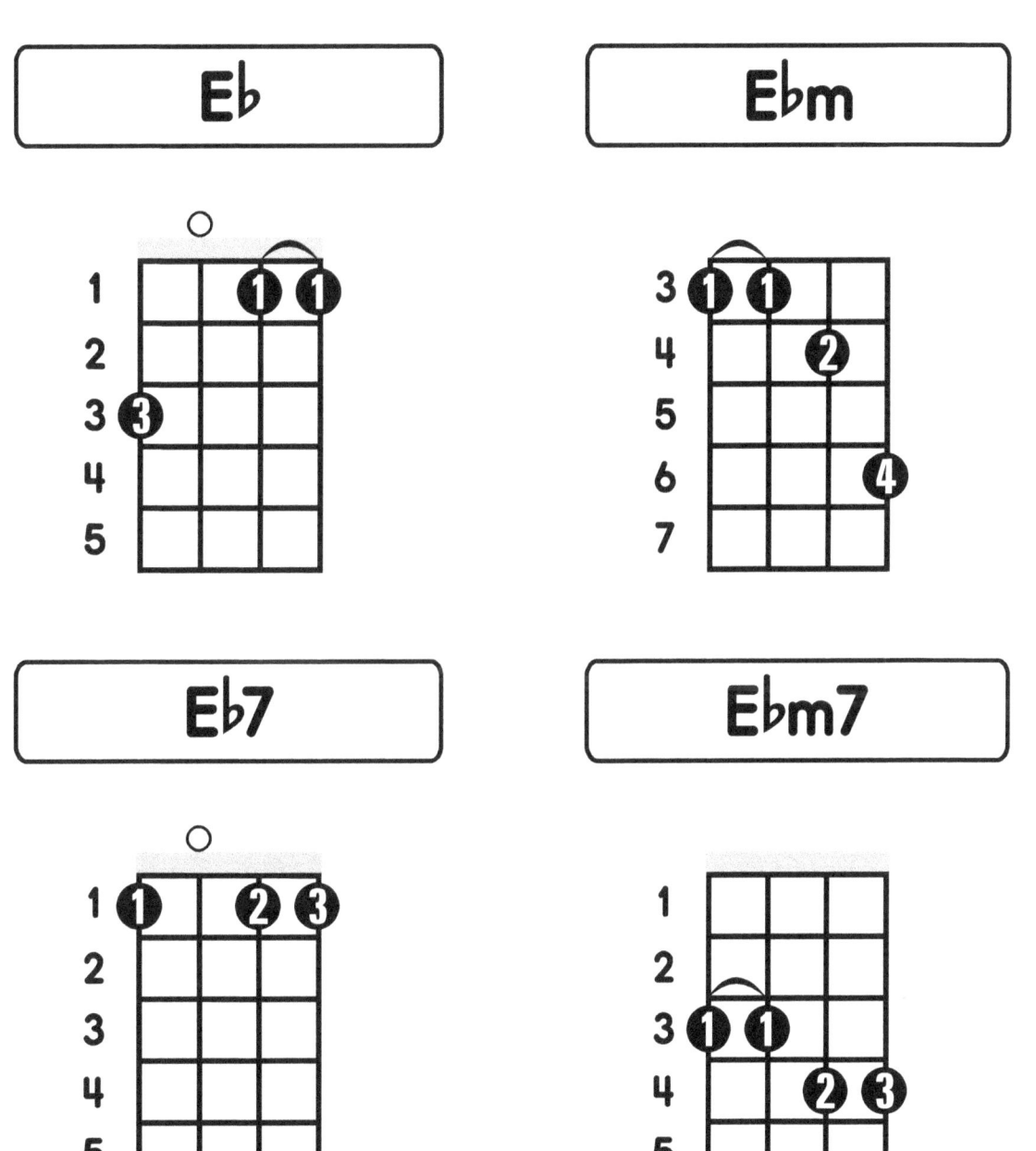

D# / E♭ Chords

E♭5
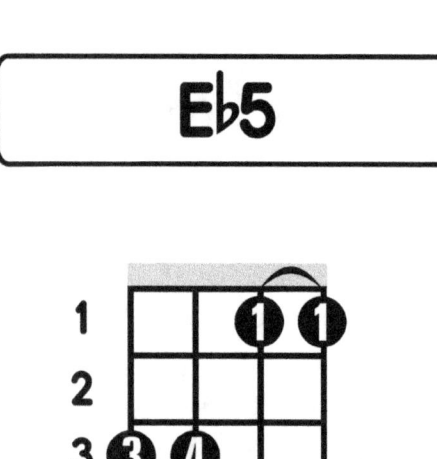

E♭6
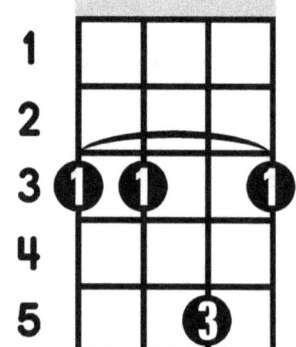

E♭m6
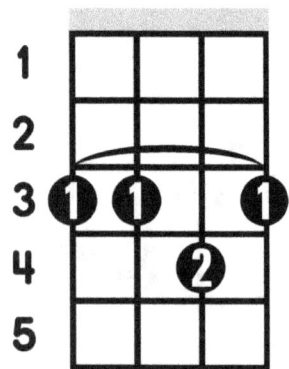

E♭maj7
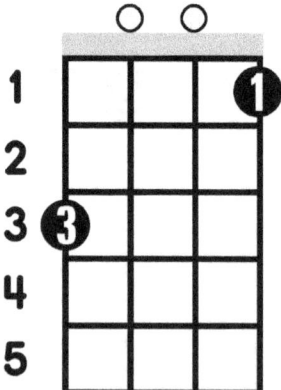

D# / E♭ Chords

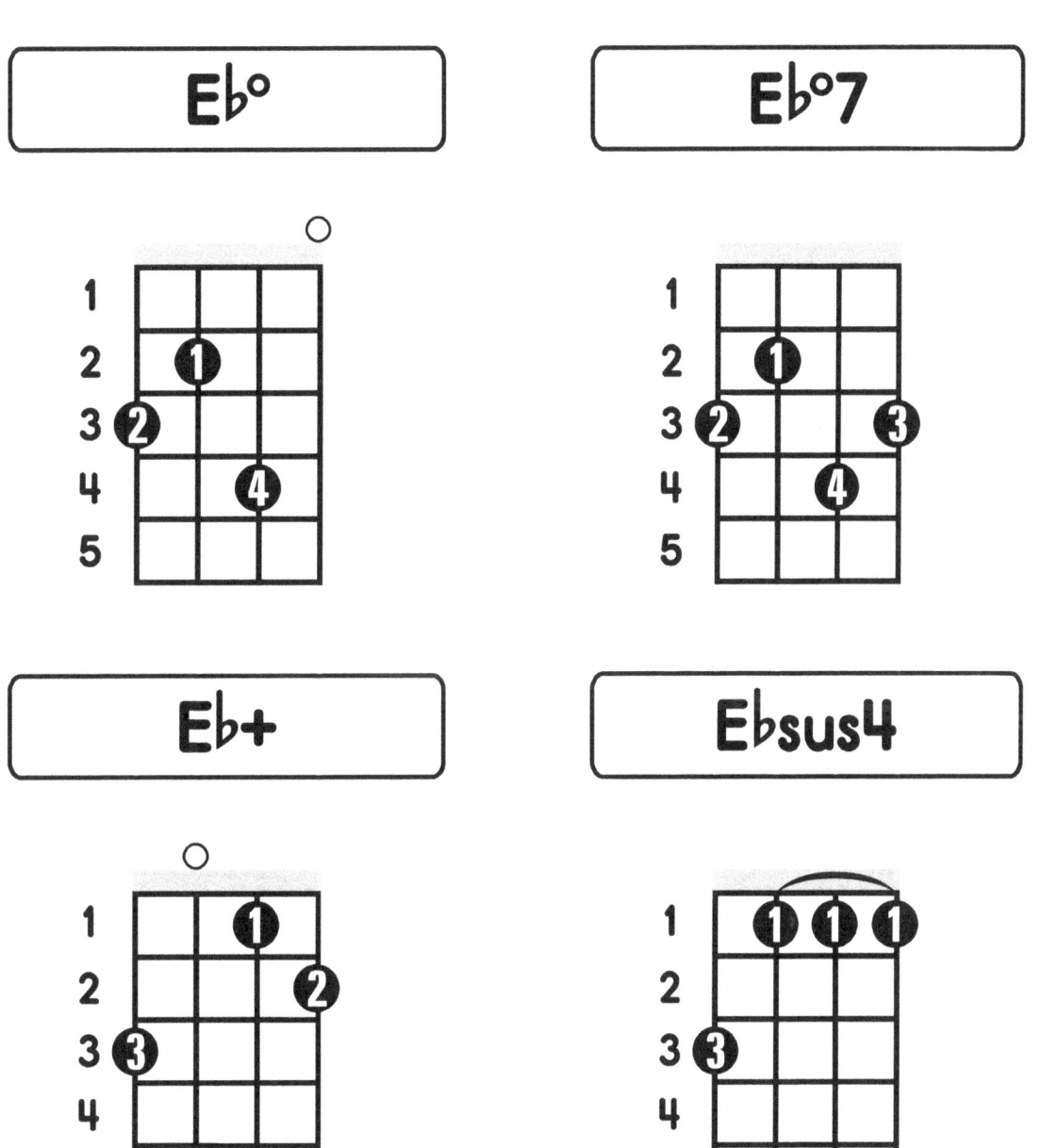

D# / E♭ Chords

E♭add9

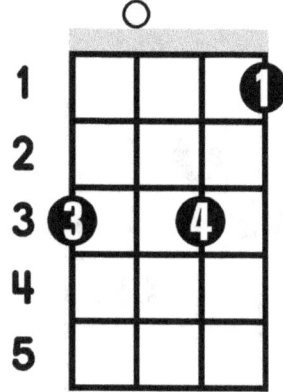

E♭madd9

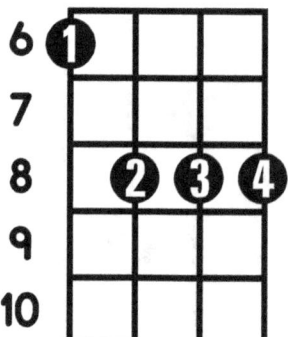

E♭m7-5

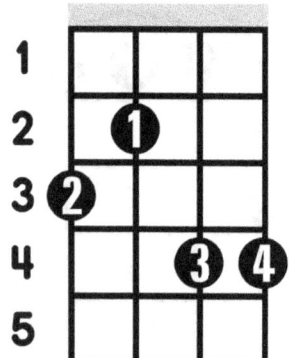

E♭7sus4

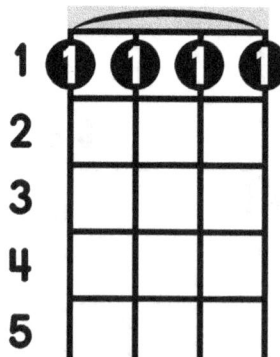

D♯ / E♭ Chords

E♭sus2

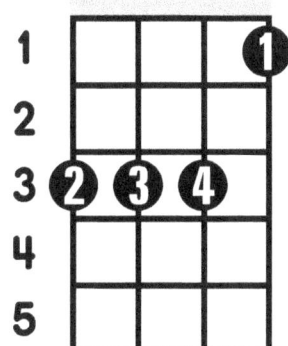

E♭m(maj7)

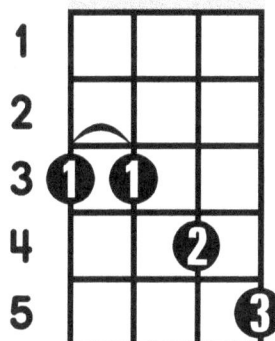

E♭7-5

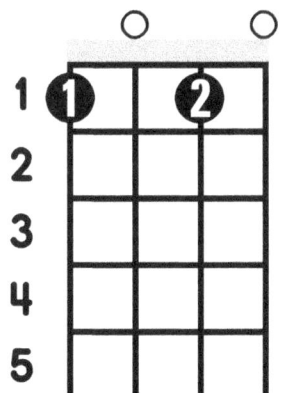

E♭7+5

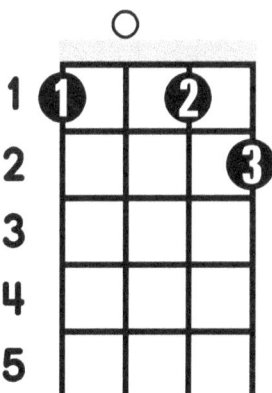

D# / E♭ Chords

E♭7-9
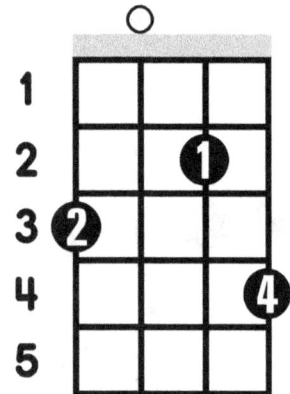

E♭7+9
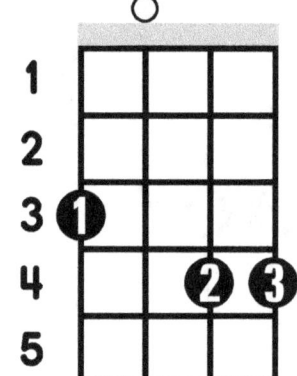

E♭-5
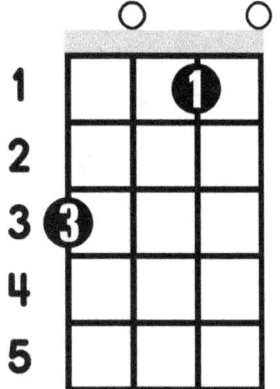

E♭9
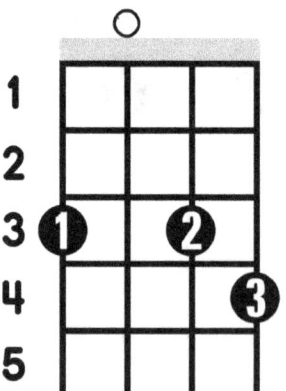

D♯ / E♭ Chords

E♭m9
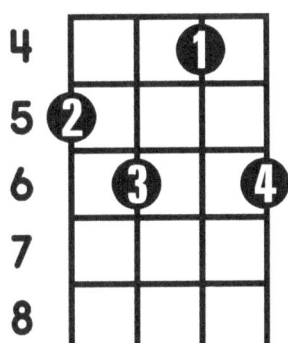

E♭maj9
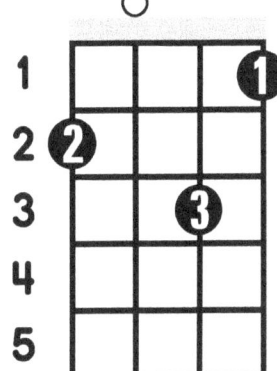

E♭11
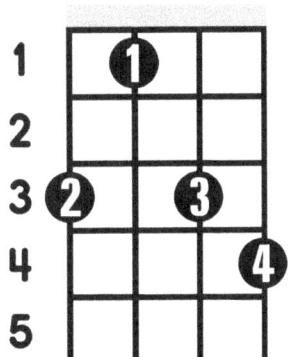

E♭13
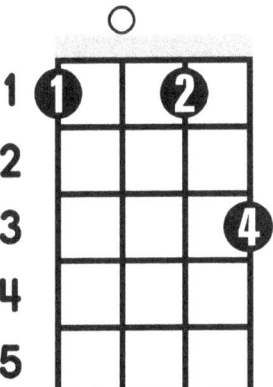

E Chords

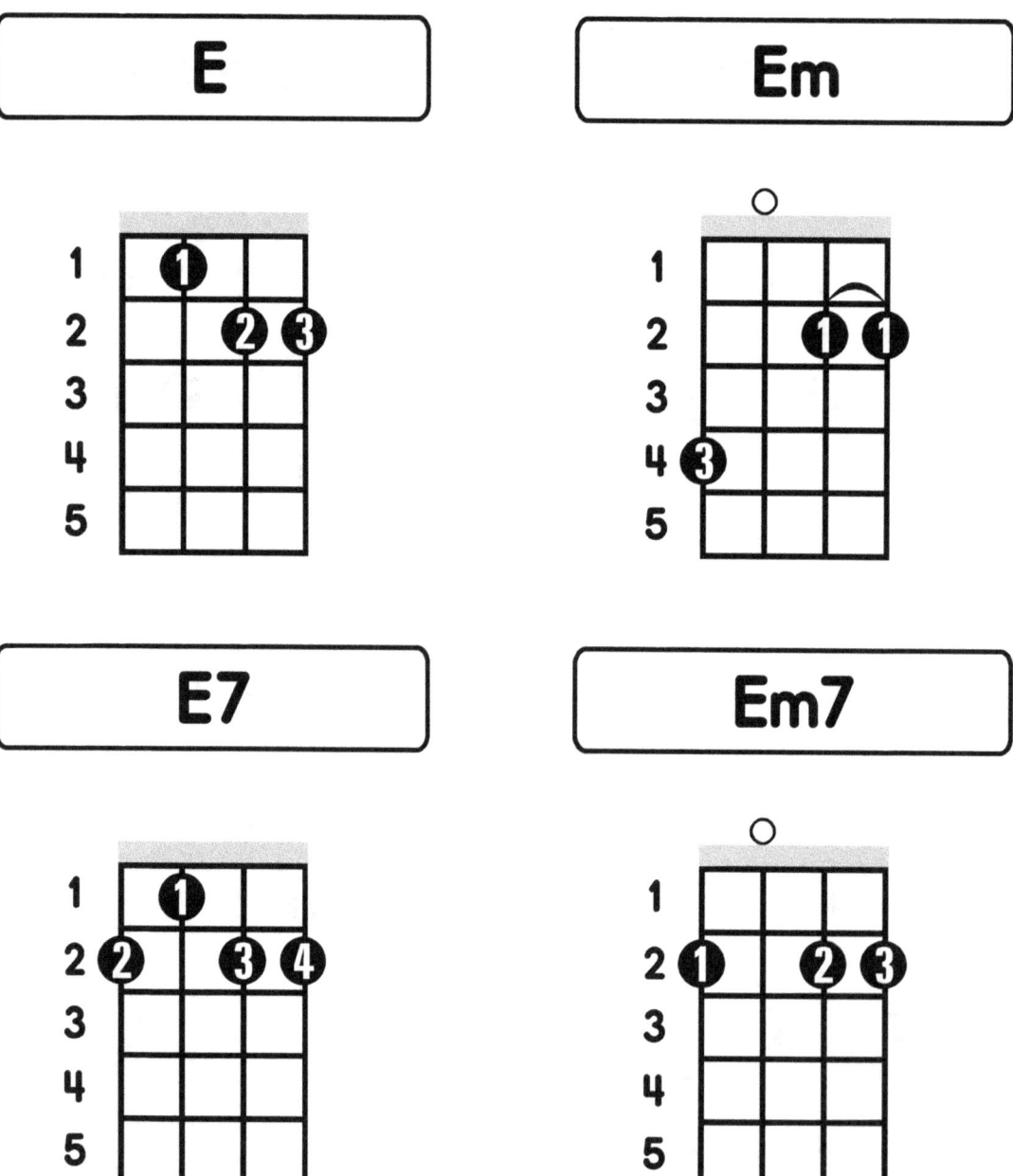

E Chords

E5
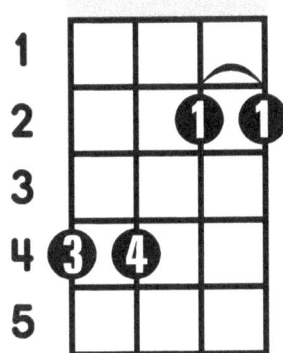

E6
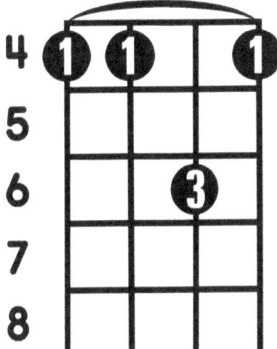

Em6
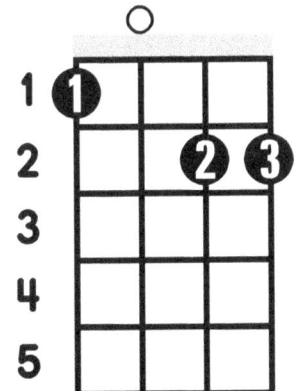

Emaj7
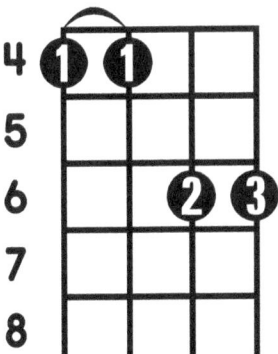

E Chords

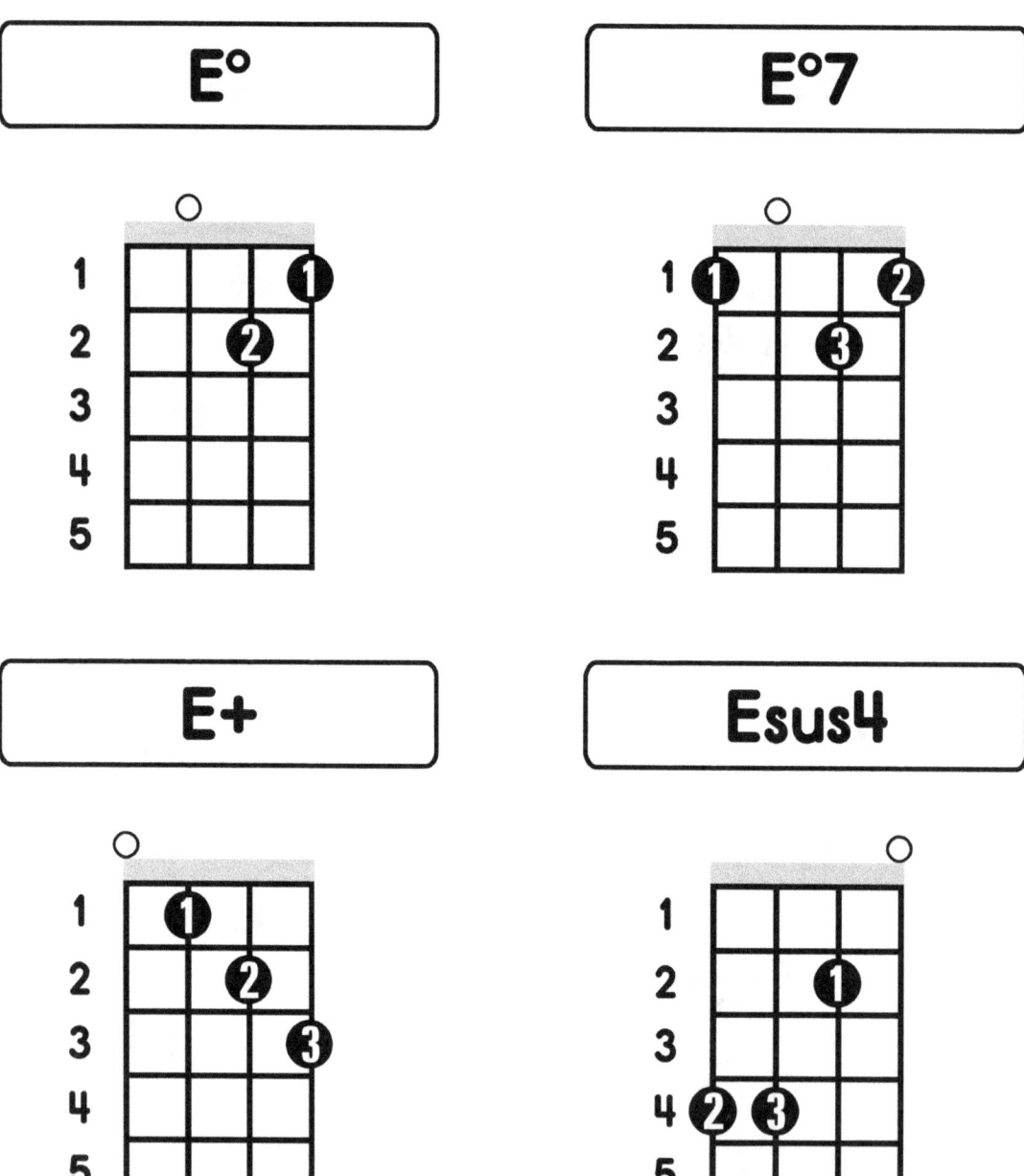

E Chords

Eadd9
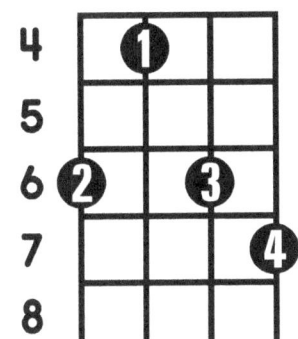

Emadd9
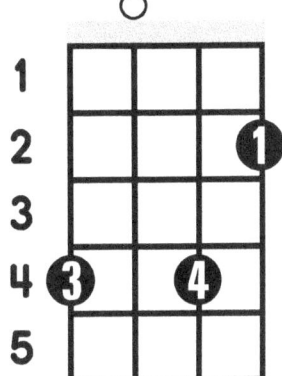

Em7-5
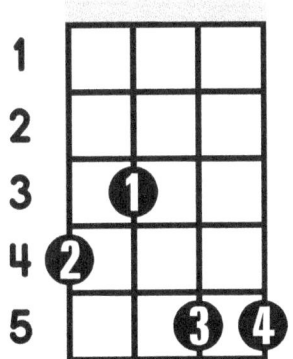

E7sus4
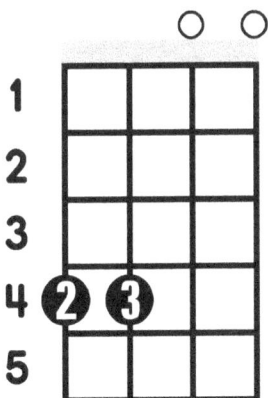

E Chords

Esus2
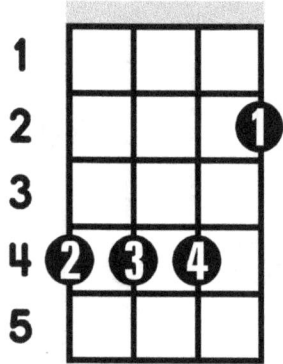

Em(maj7)
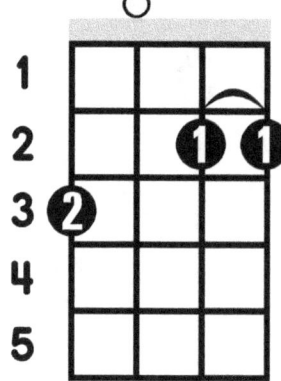

E7-5
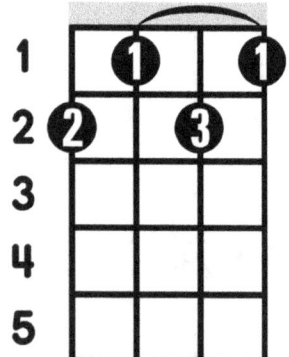

E7+5
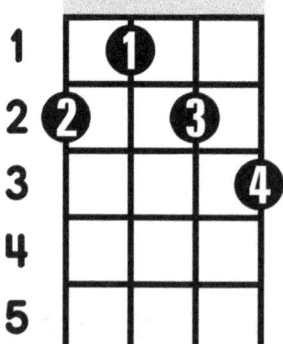

E Chords

E7-9
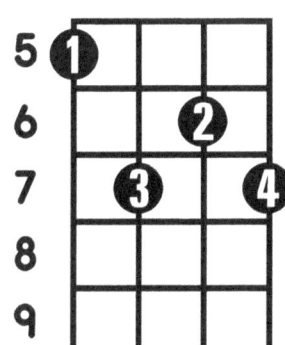

E7+9
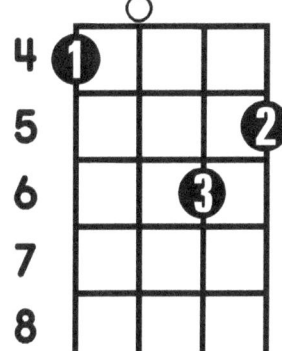

E-5
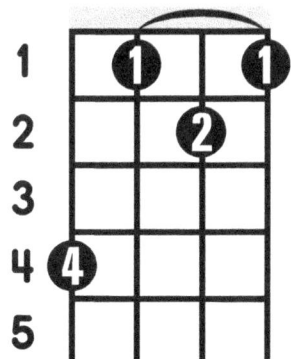

E9
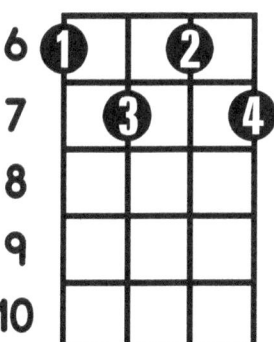

E Chords

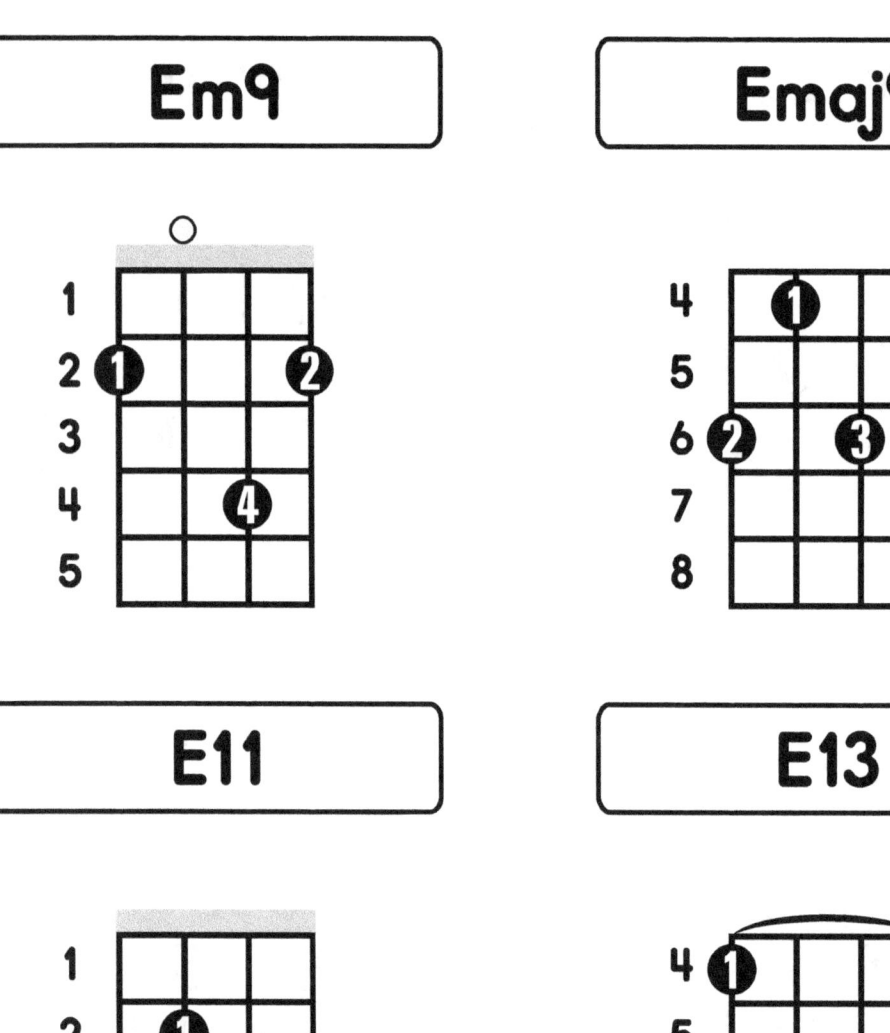

F Chords

F

Fm

F7

Fm7

F Chords

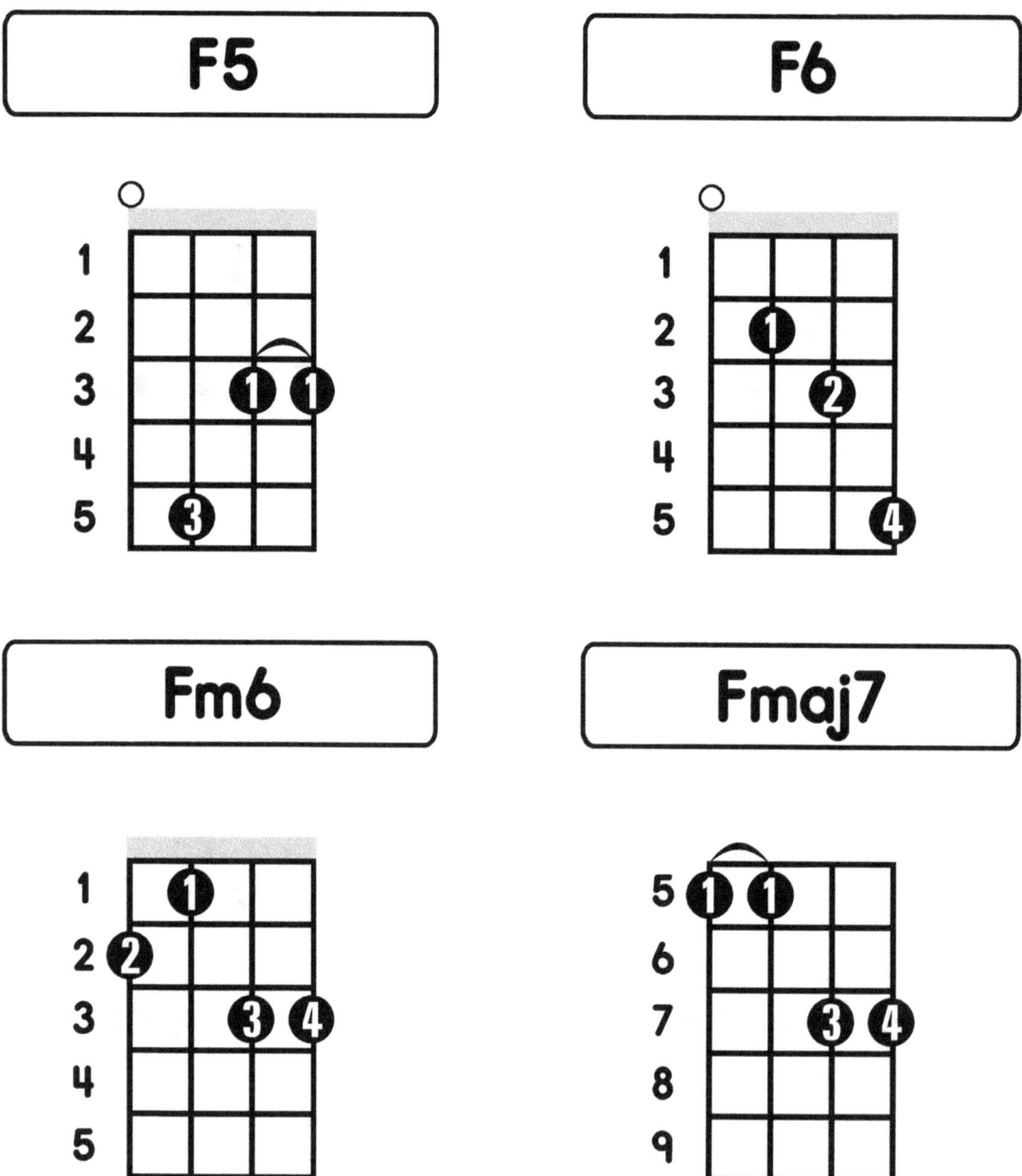

F Chords

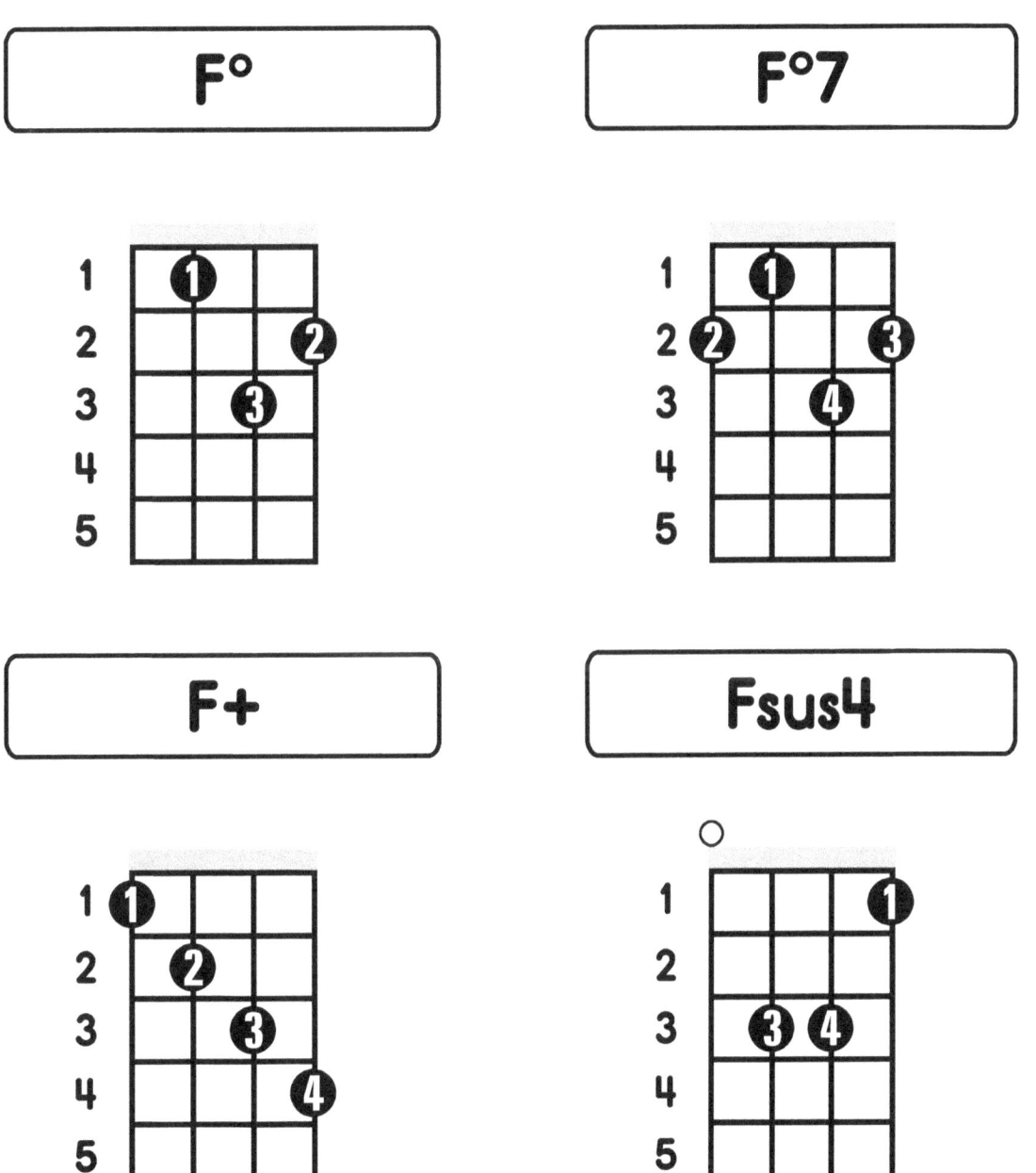

F Chords

Fadd9

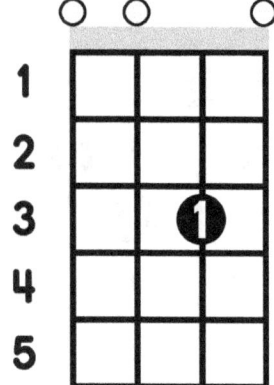

Fmadd9

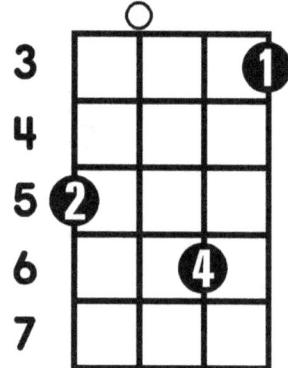

Fm7-5

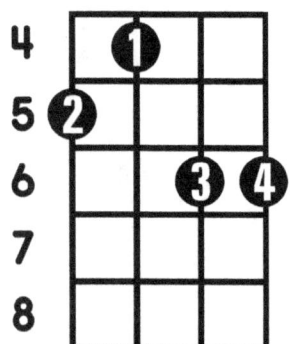

F7sus4

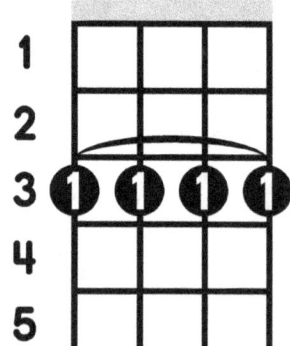

F Chords

Fsus2

Fm(maj7)

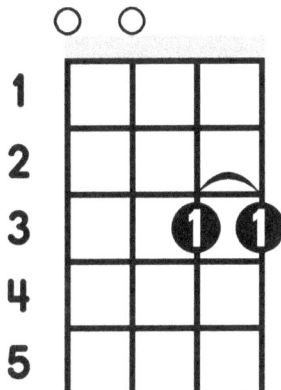

F7-5

F7+5

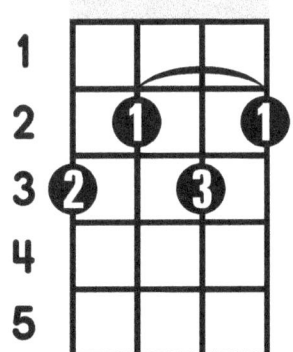
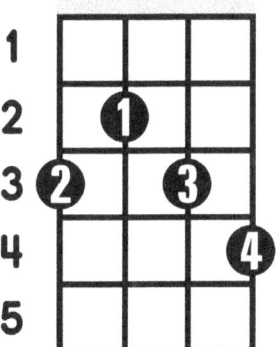

F Chords

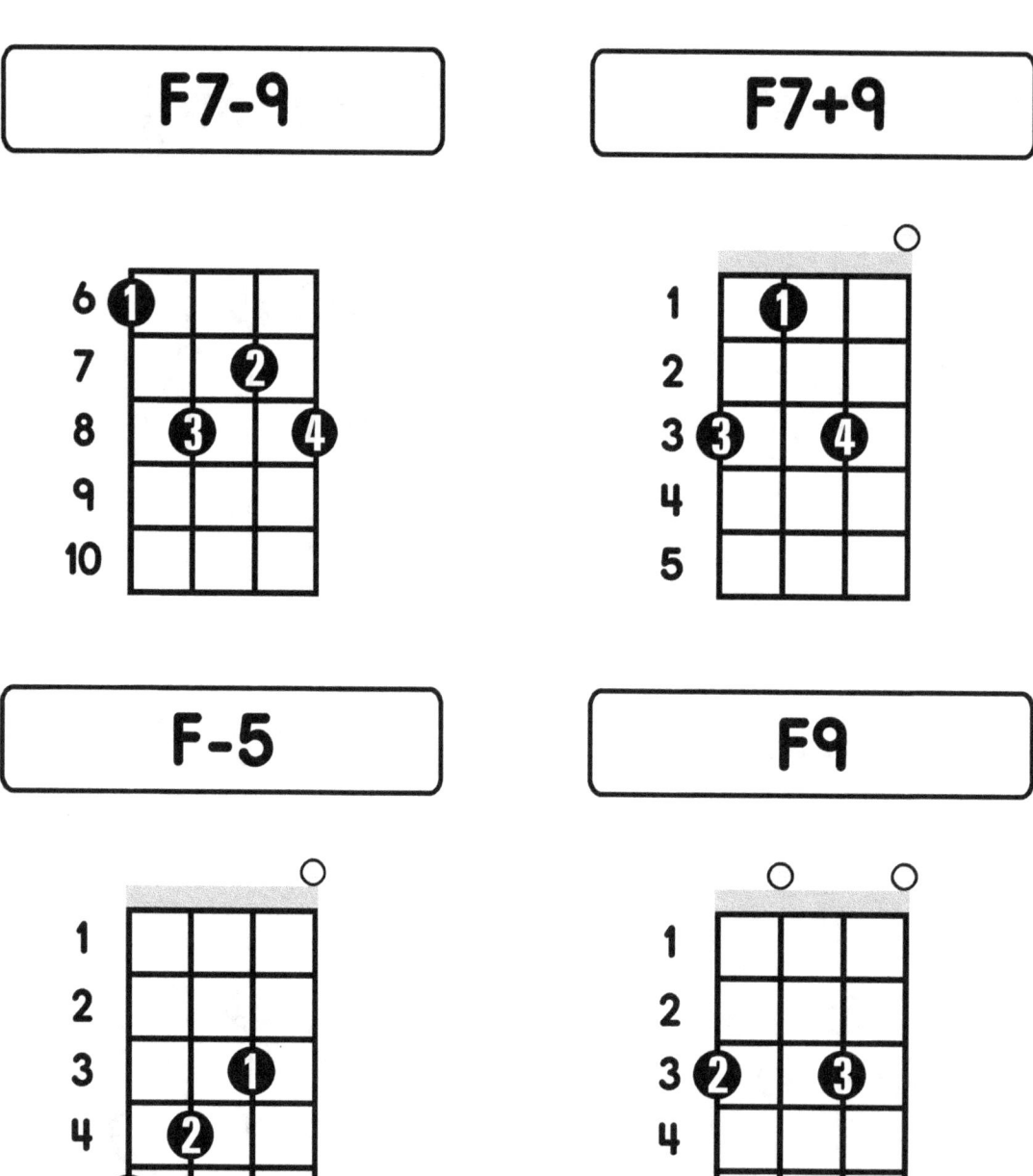

F Chords

Fm9
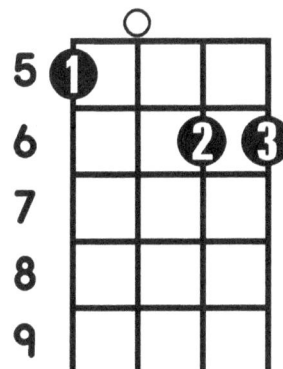

Fmaj9
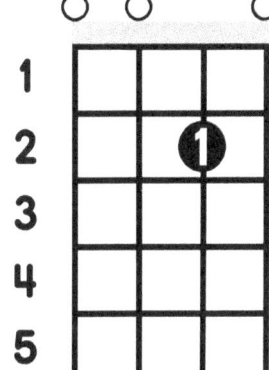

F11
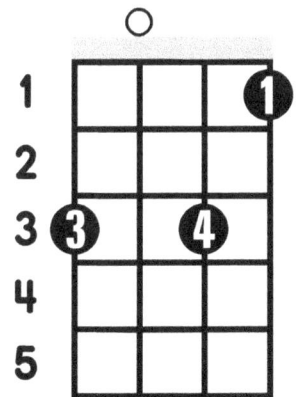

F13
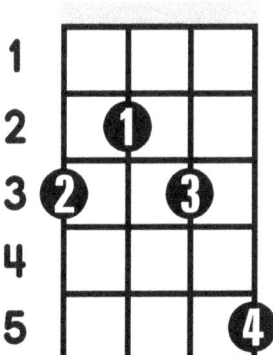

F# / G♭ Chords

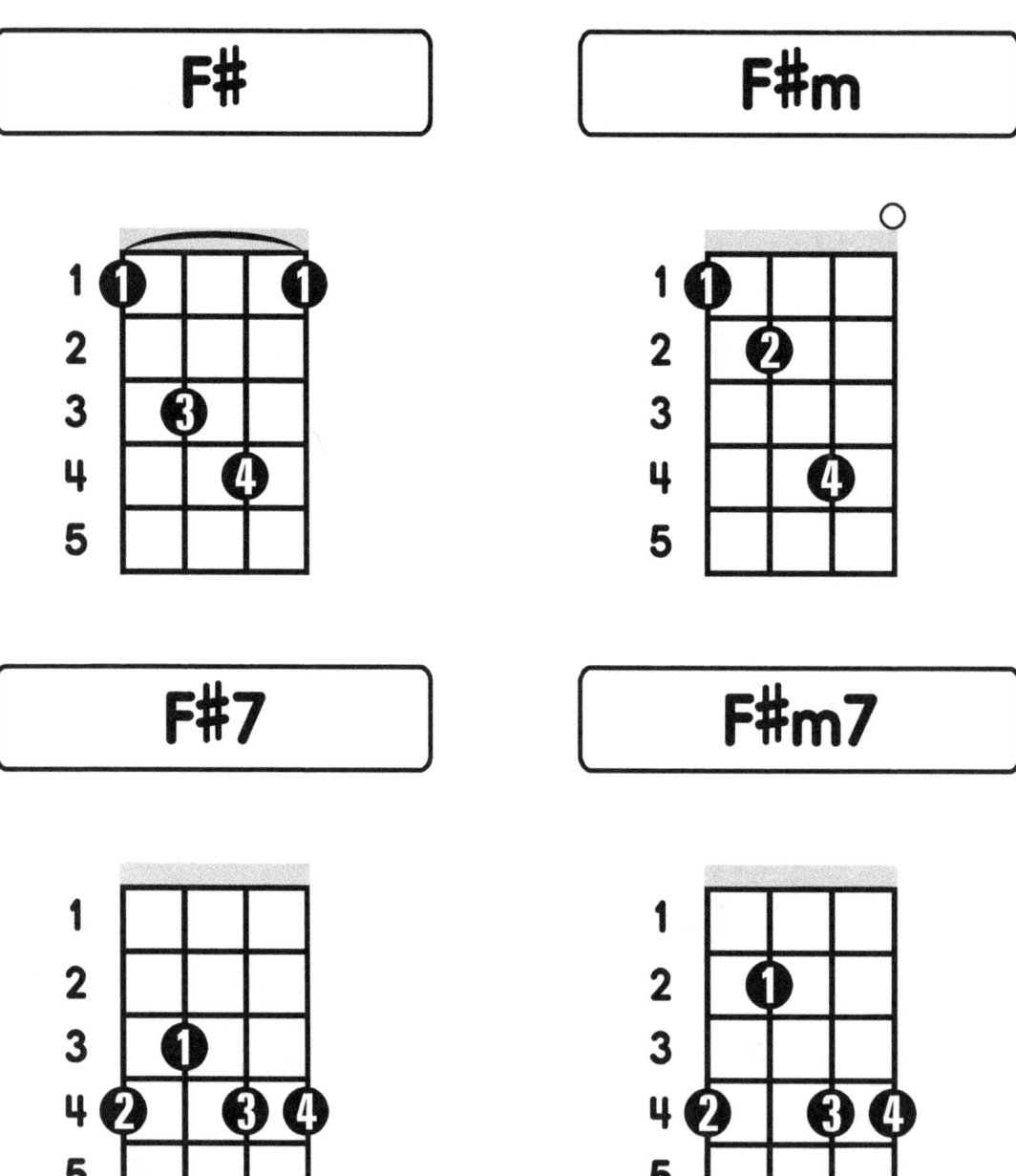

F# / G♭ Chords

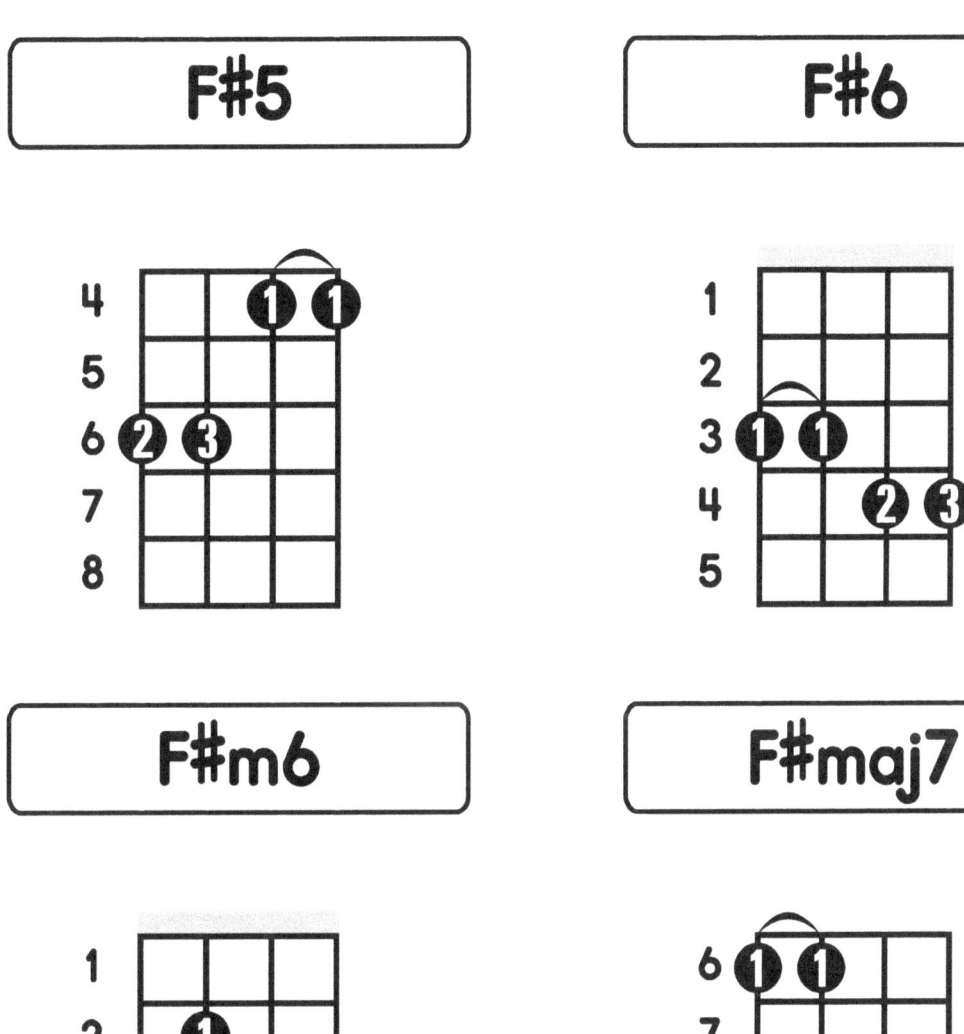

F# / G♭ Chords

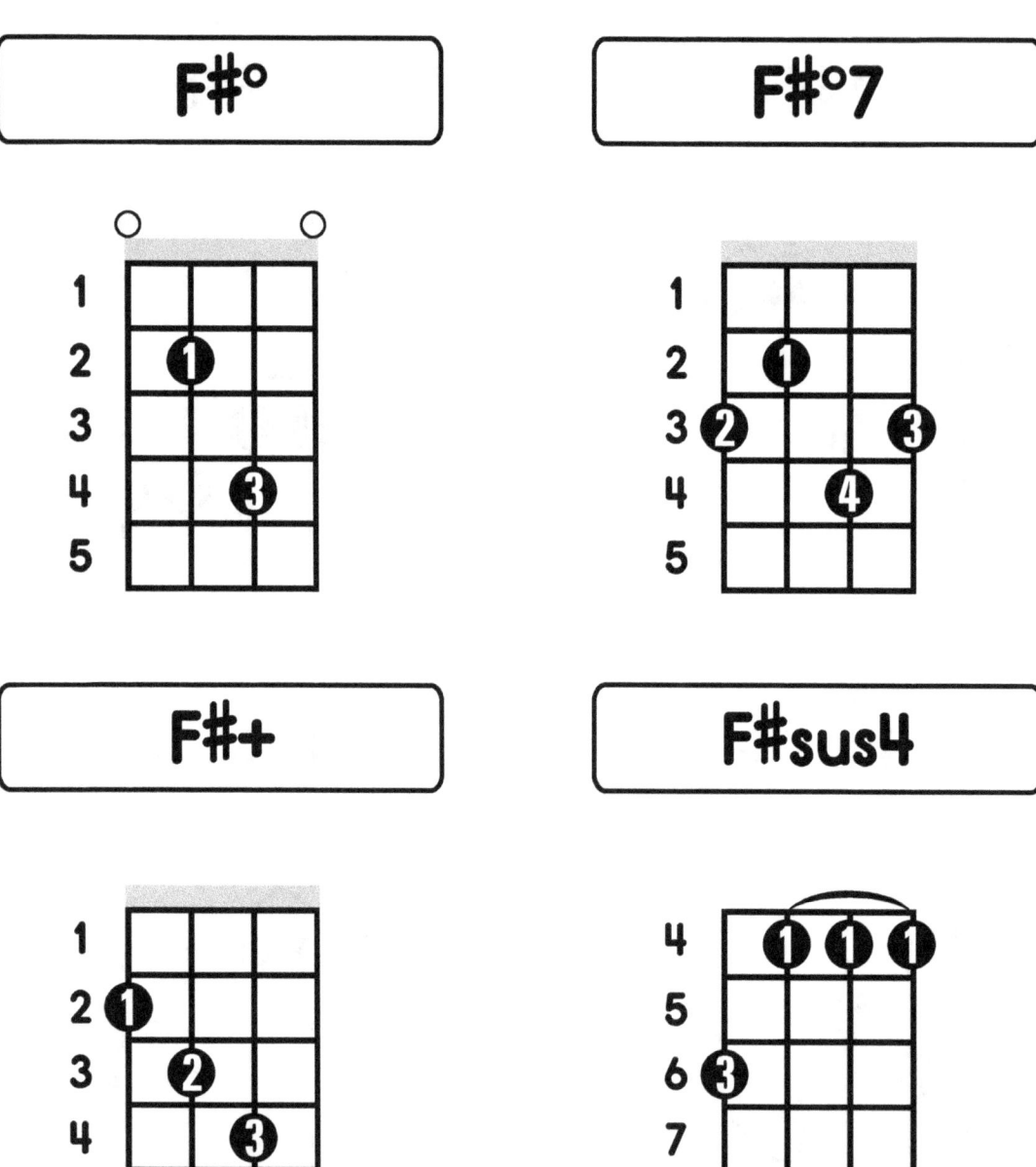

F# / G♭ Chords

F#add9
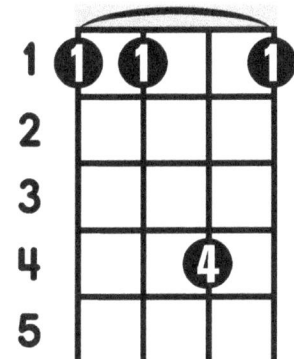

F#madd9
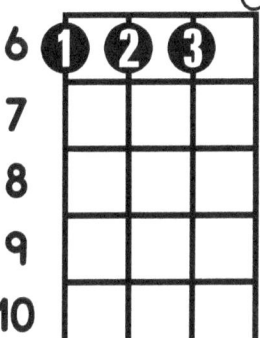

F#m7-5
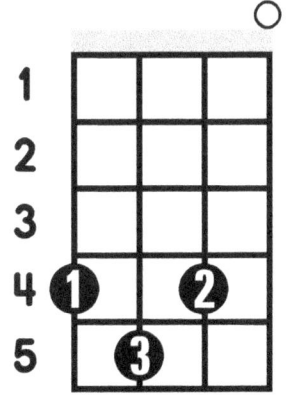

F#7sus4
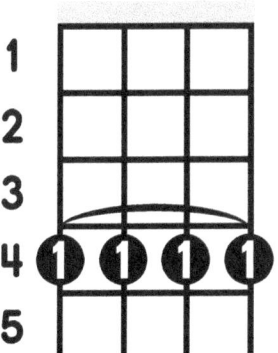

F# / G♭ Chords

F#sus2

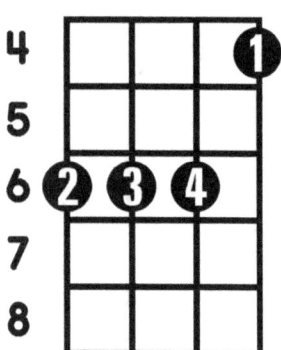

F#m(maj7)

F#7-5

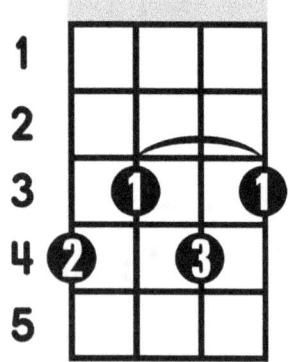

F#7+5

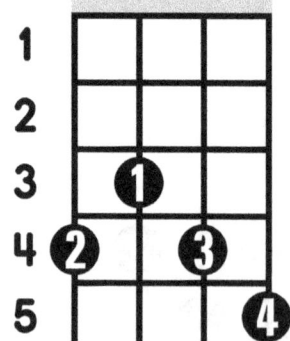

F# / G♭ Chords

F#7-9
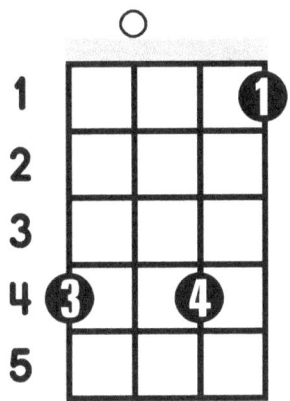

F#7+9
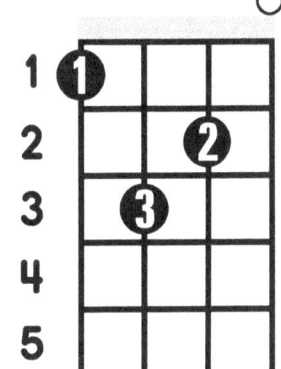

F#-5
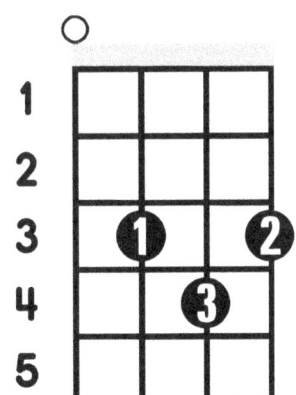

F#9
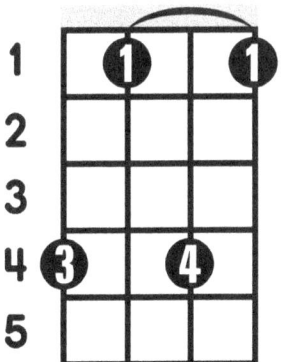

F# / Gb Chords

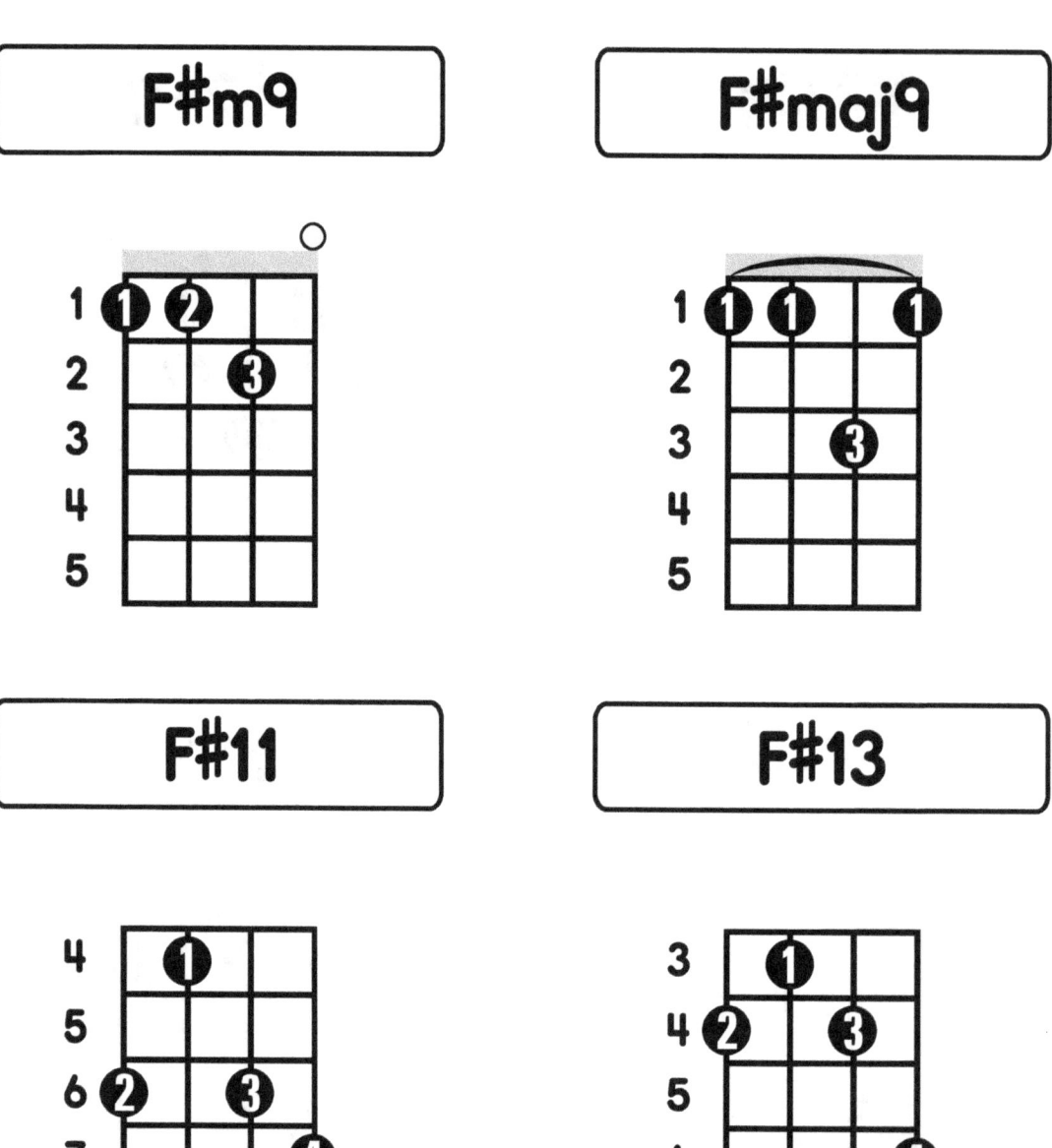

G Chords

G

Gm

G7

Gm7

G Chords

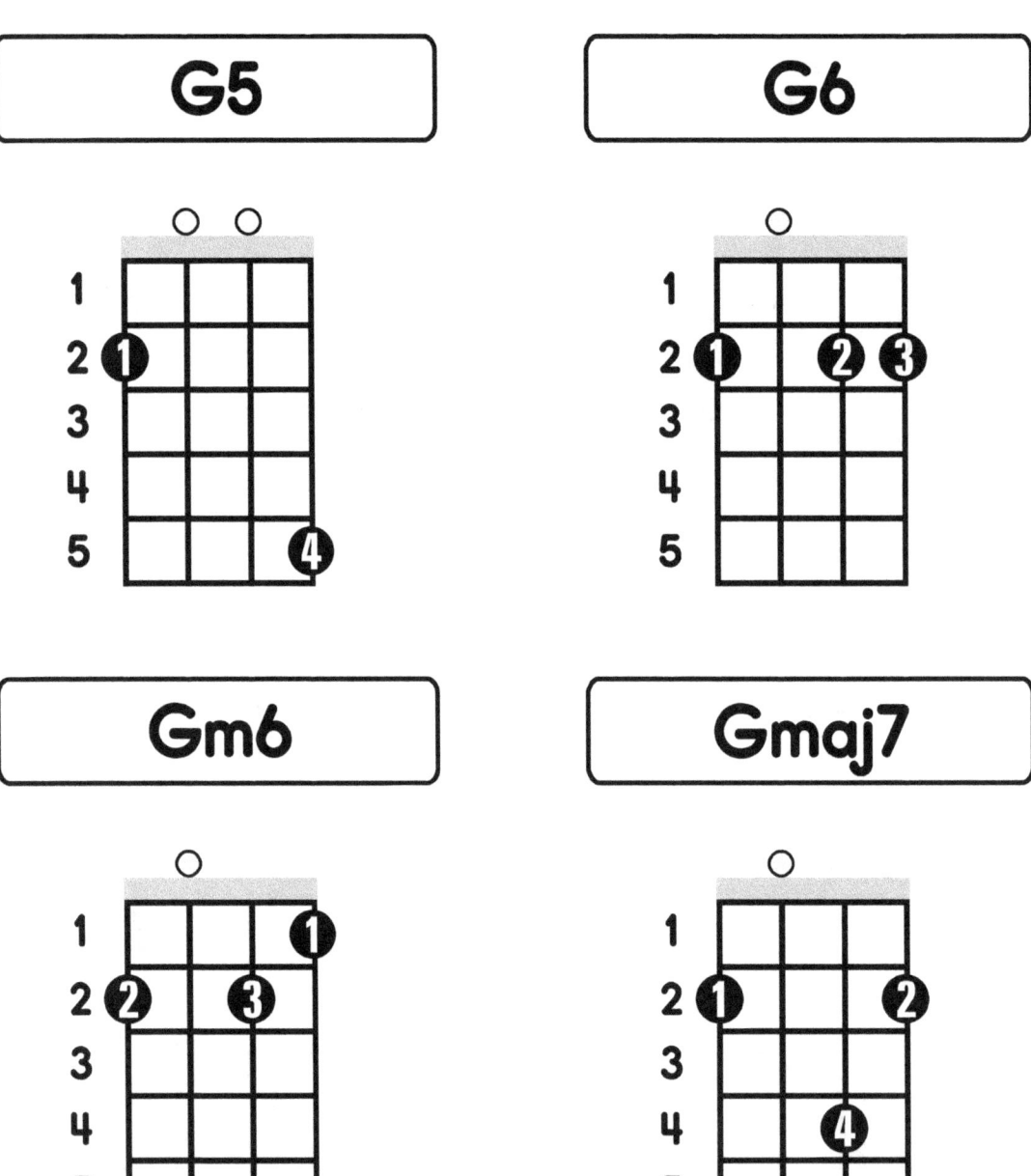

G Chords

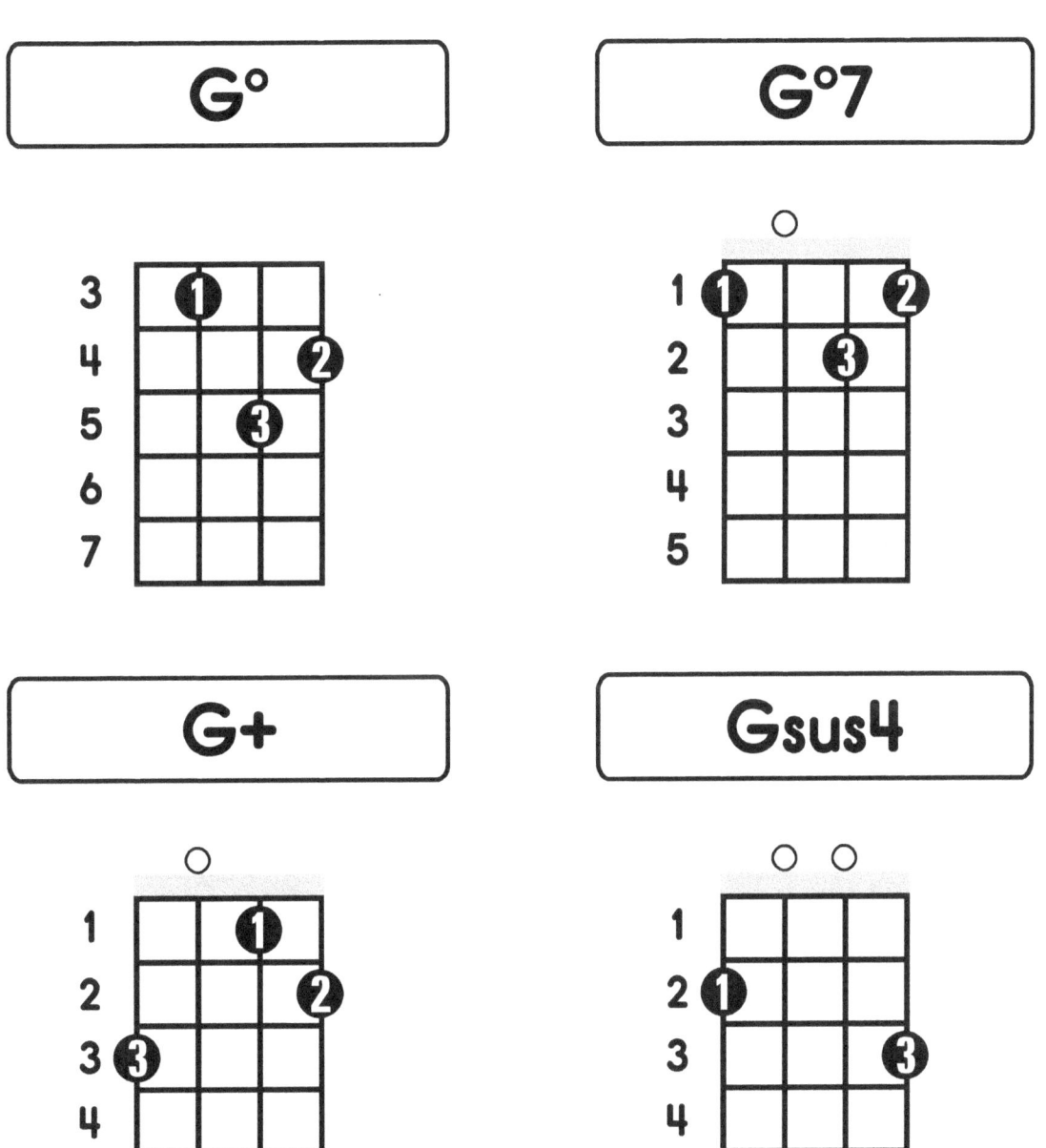

G Chords

Gadd9
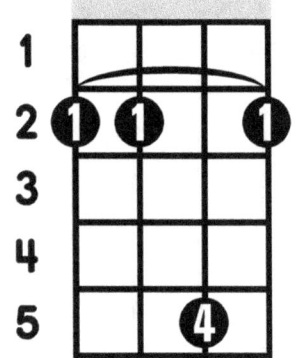

Gmadd9
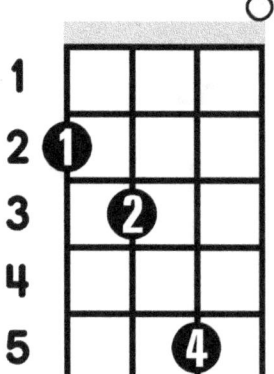

Gm7-5
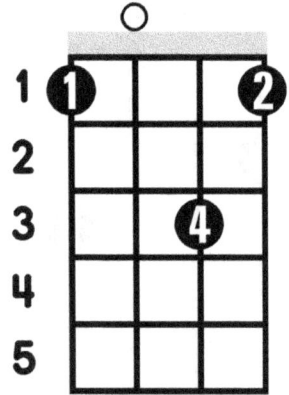

G7sus4
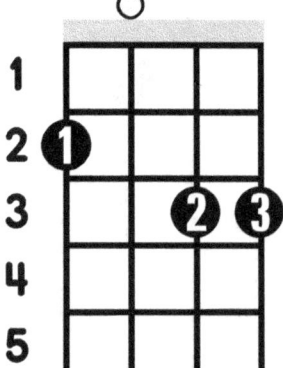

G Chords

Gsus2
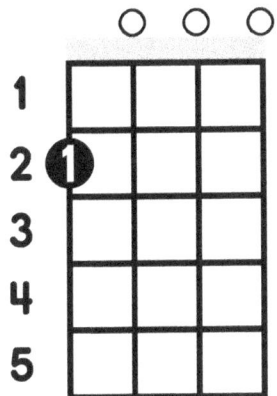

Gm(maj7)
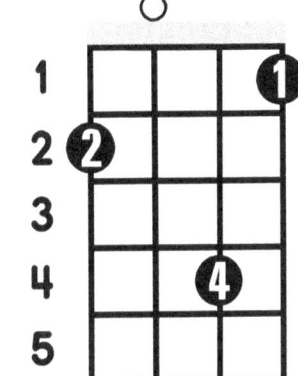

G7-5
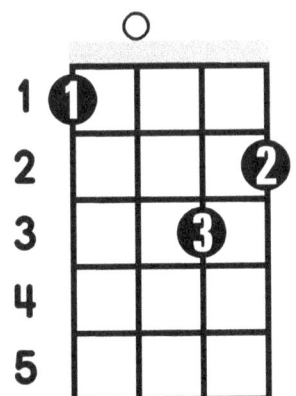

G7+5
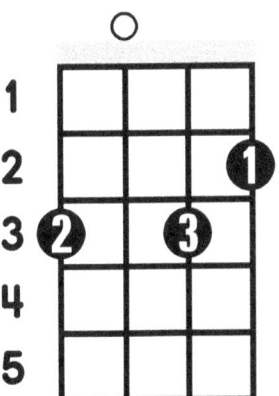

G Chords

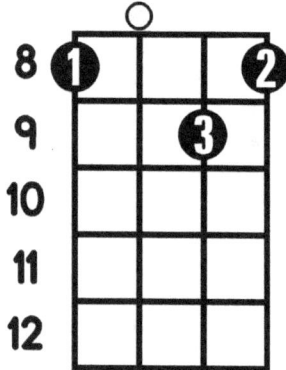
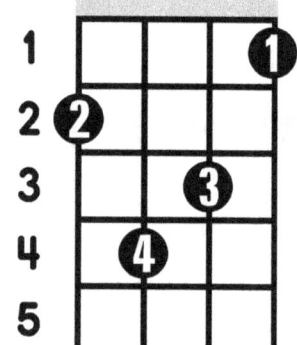

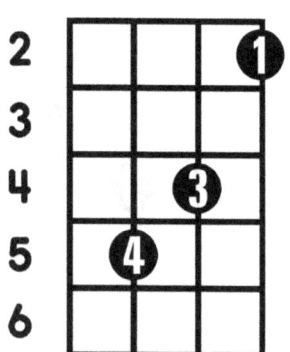
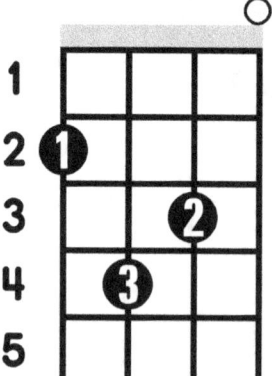

G Chords

Gm9
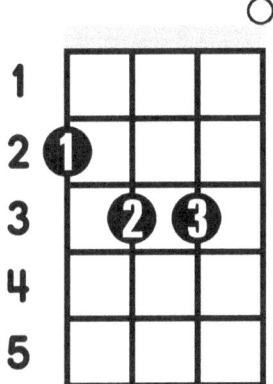

Gmaj9
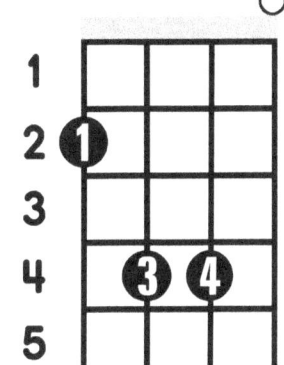

G11
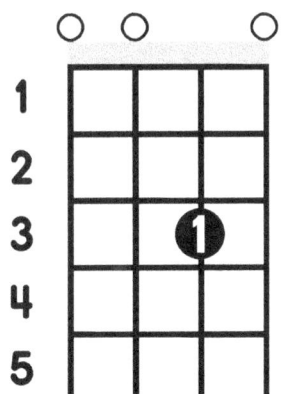

G13
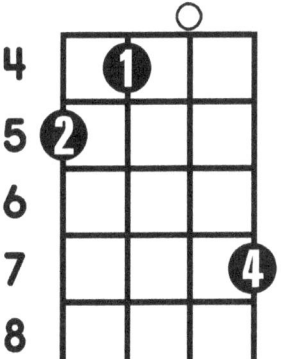

G# / A♭ Chords

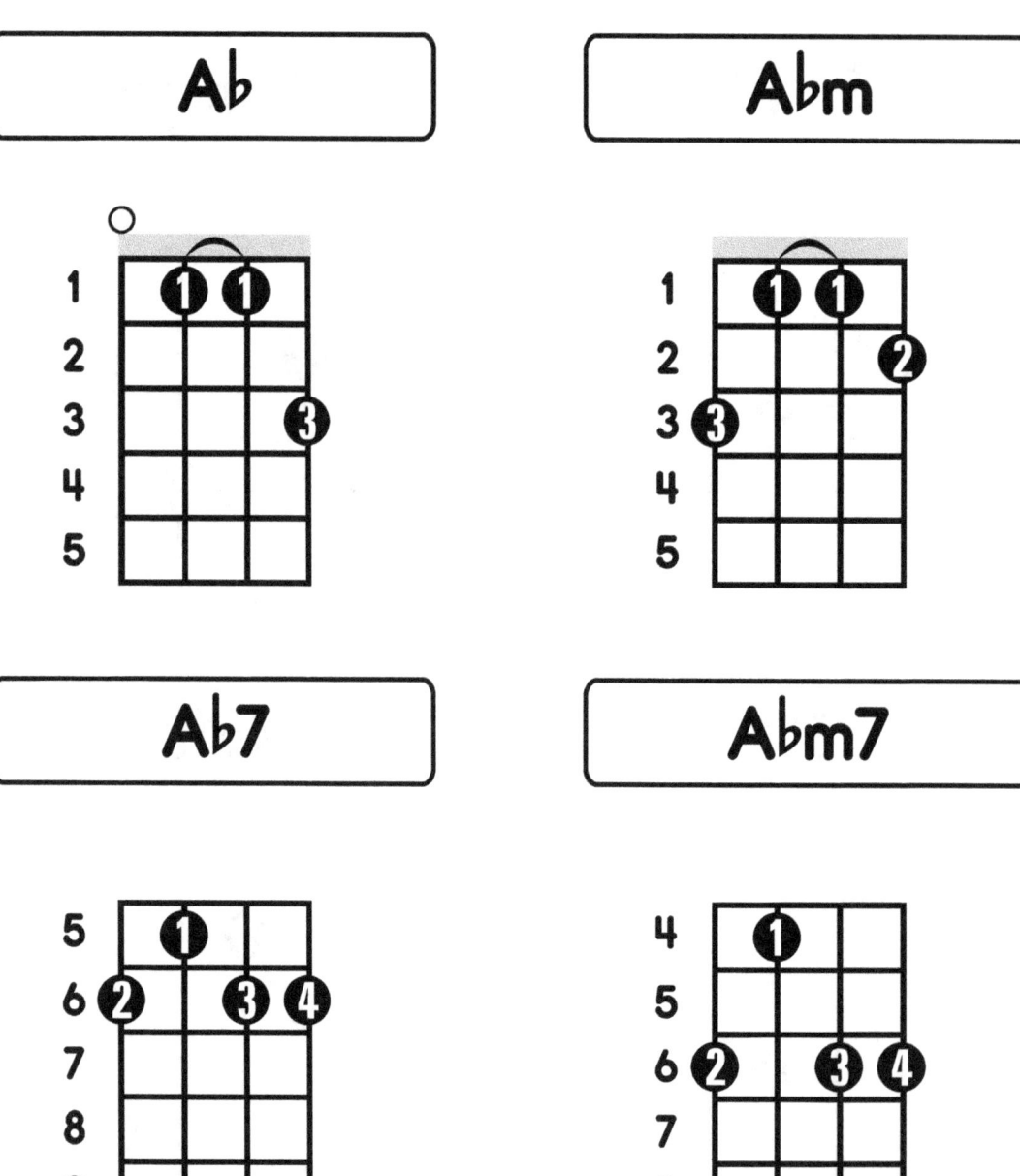

G# / A♭ Chords

A♭5

A♭6

A♭m6

A♭maj7

G# / A♭ Chords

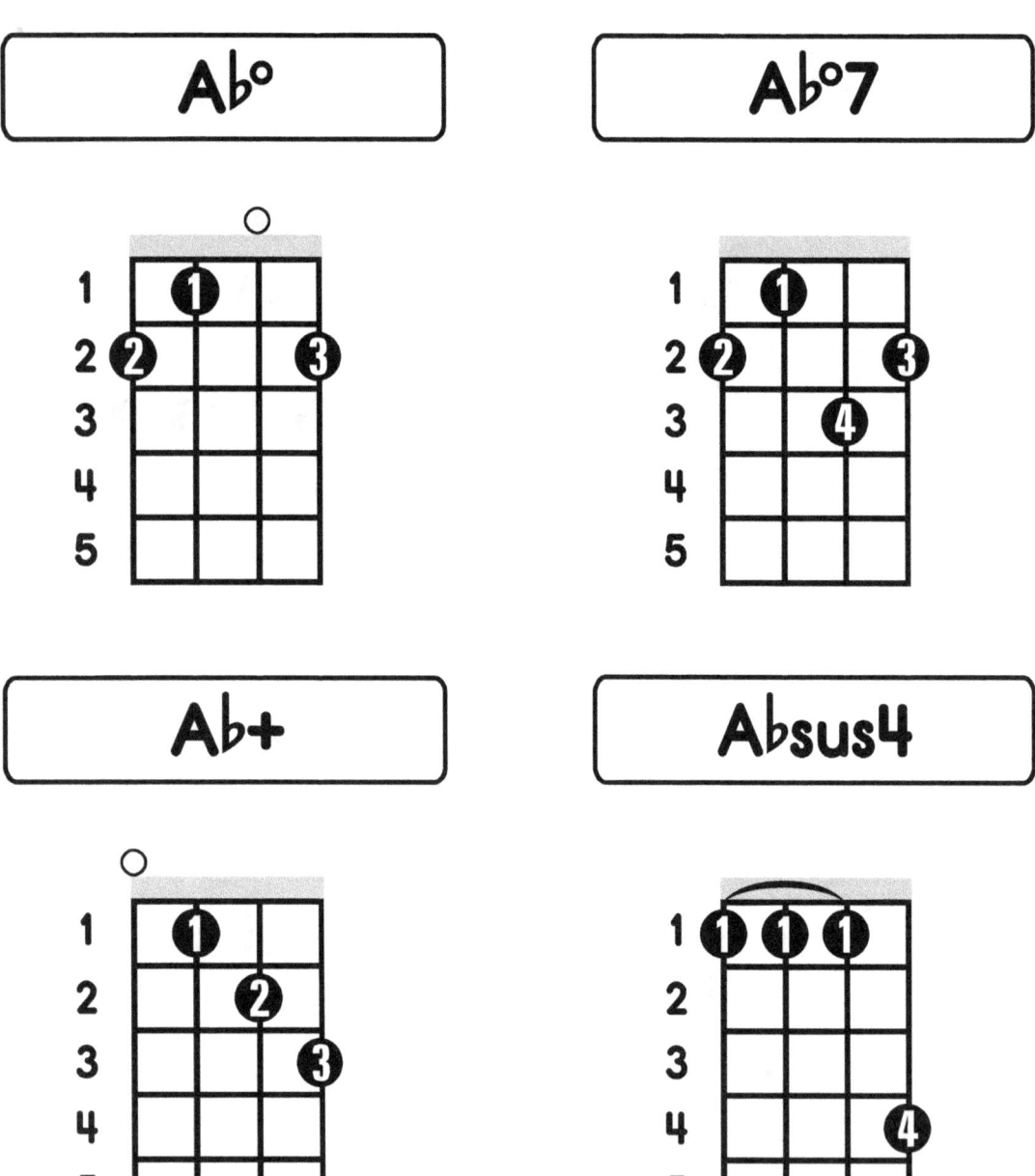

G# / A♭ Chords

A♭add9
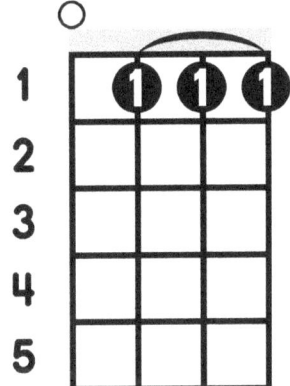

A♭madd9
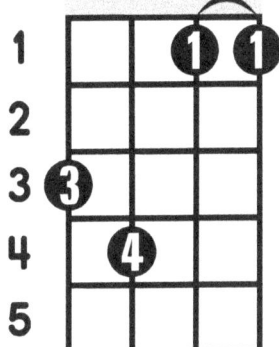

A♭m7-5
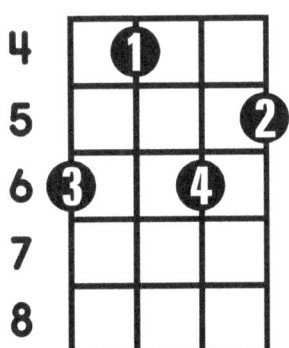

A♭7sus4
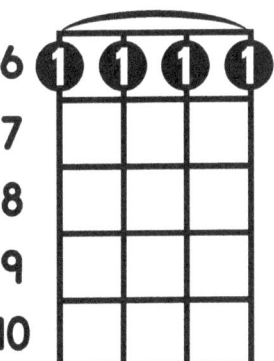

G# / A♭ Chords

A♭sus2

A♭m(maj7)

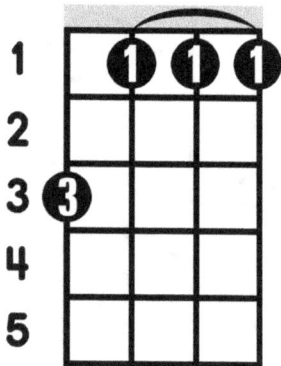

A♭7-5

A♭7+5

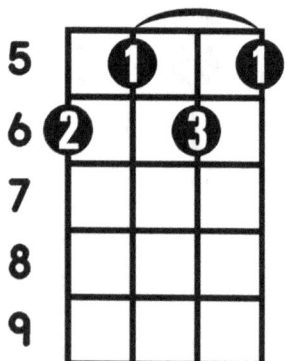
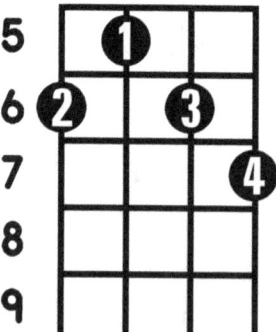

G# / A♭ Chords

A♭7-9
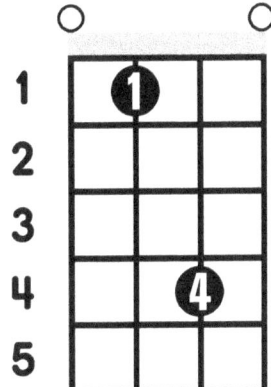

A♭7+9
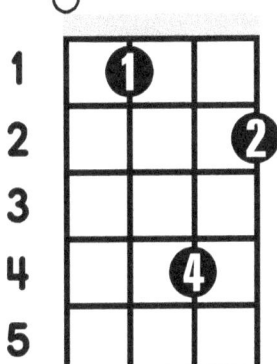

A♭-5
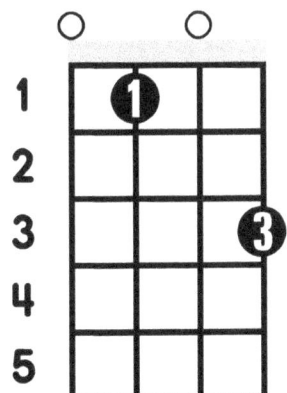

A♭9
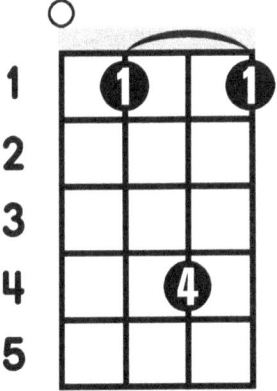

G# / A♭ Chords

A♭m9
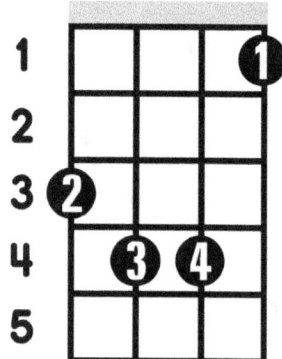

A♭maj9
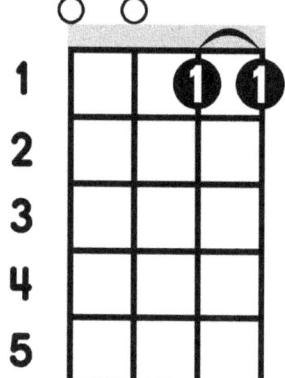

A♭11
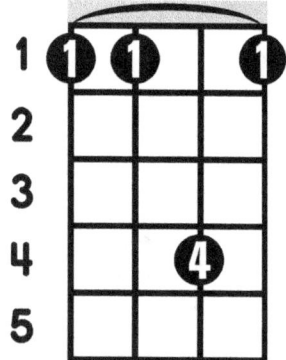

A♭13
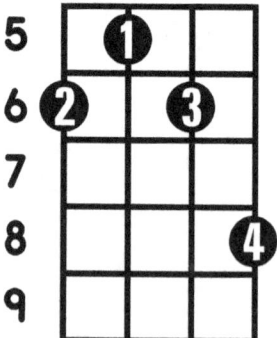

A Chords

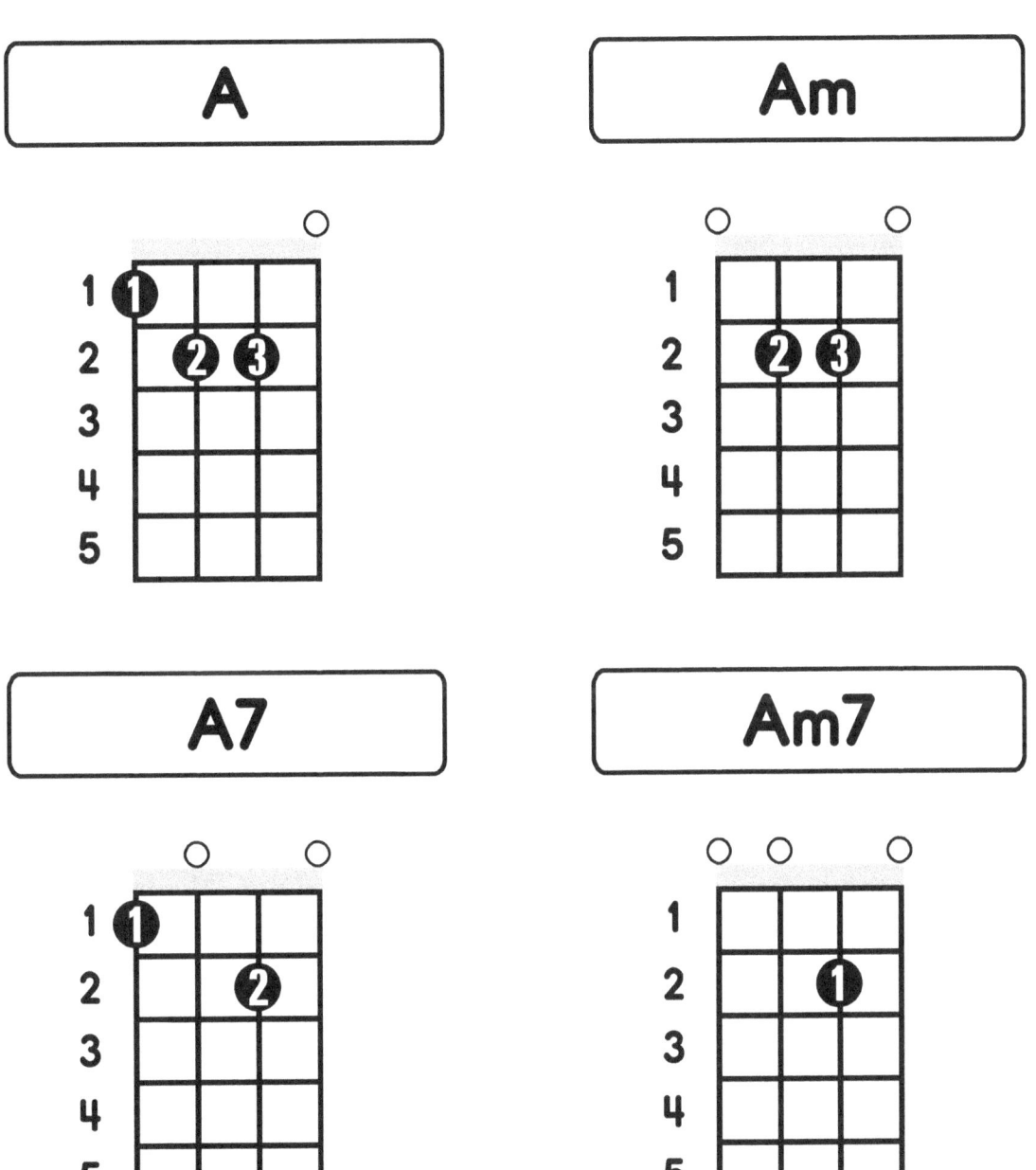

A Chords

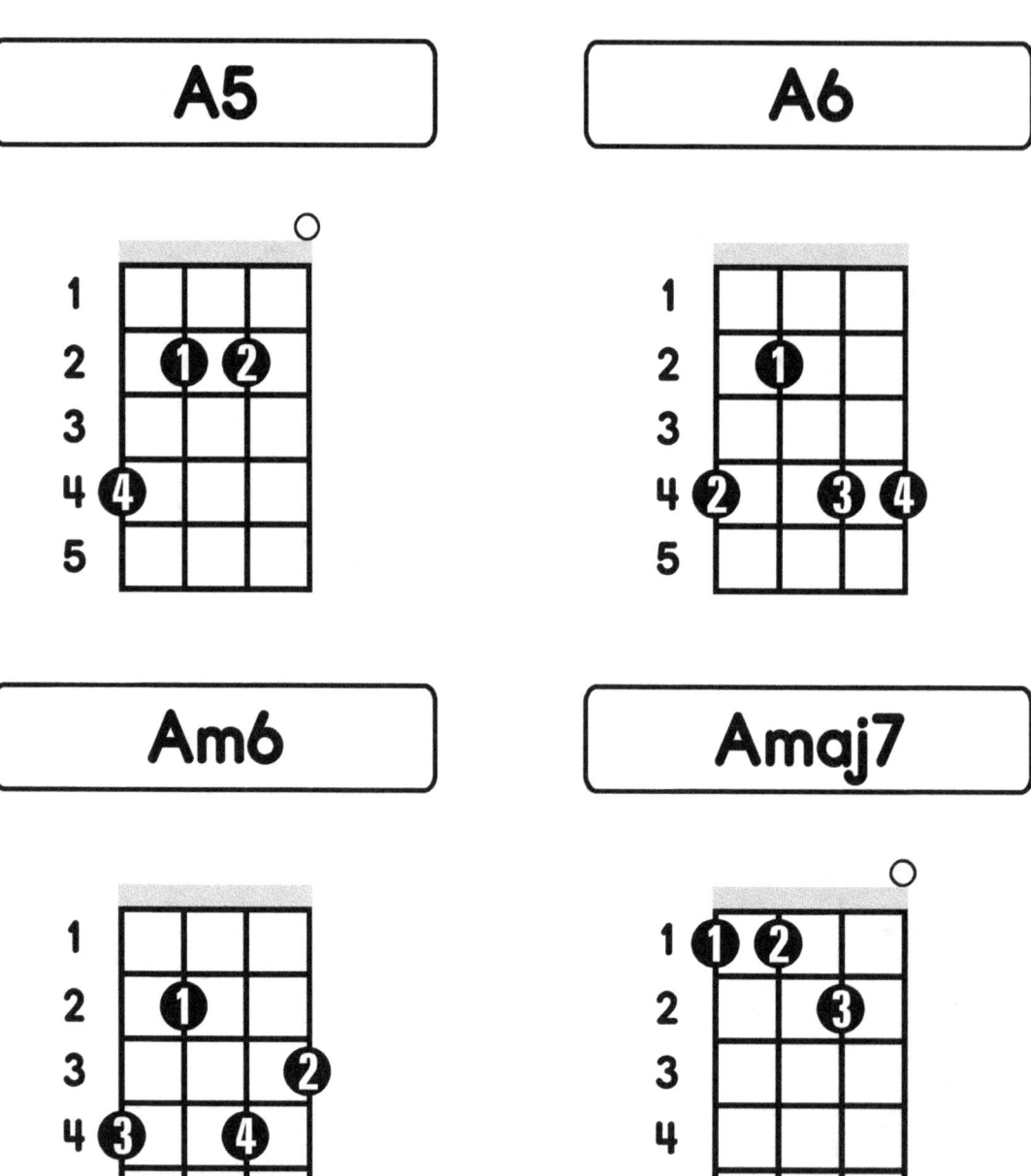

A Chords

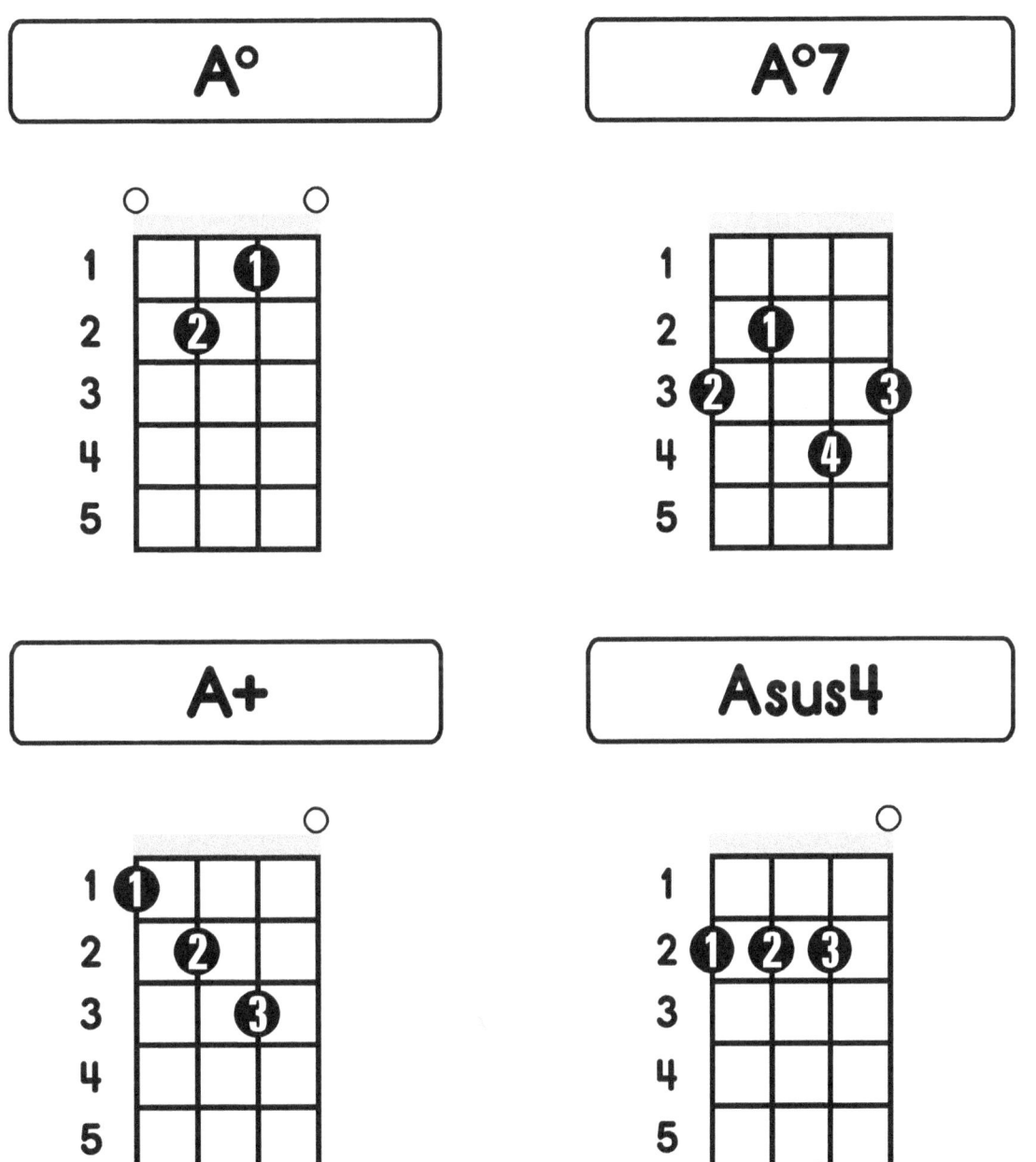

A Chords

Aadd9
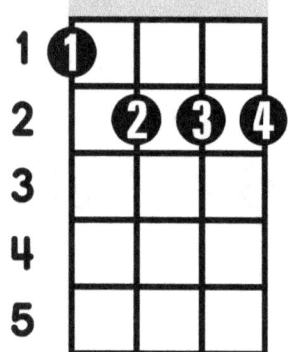

Amadd9
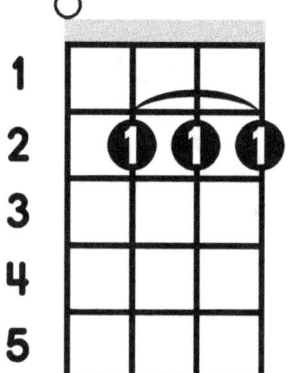

Am7-5
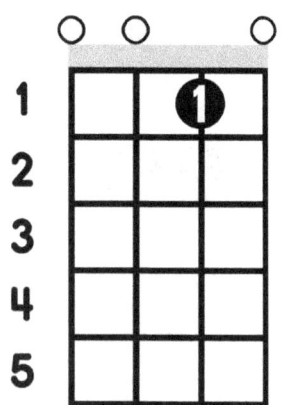

A7sus4
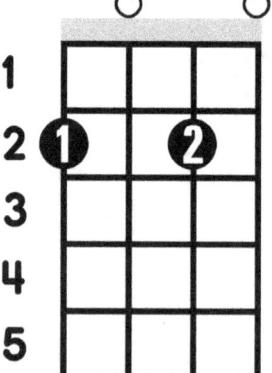

A Chords

Asus2
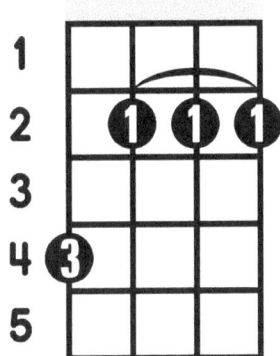

Am(maj7)
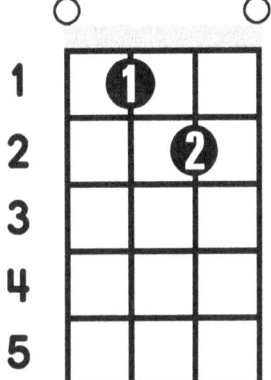

A7-5
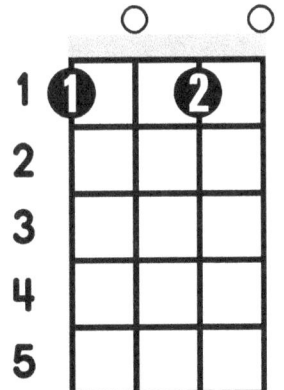

A7+5
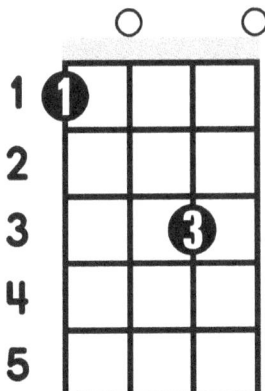

A Chords

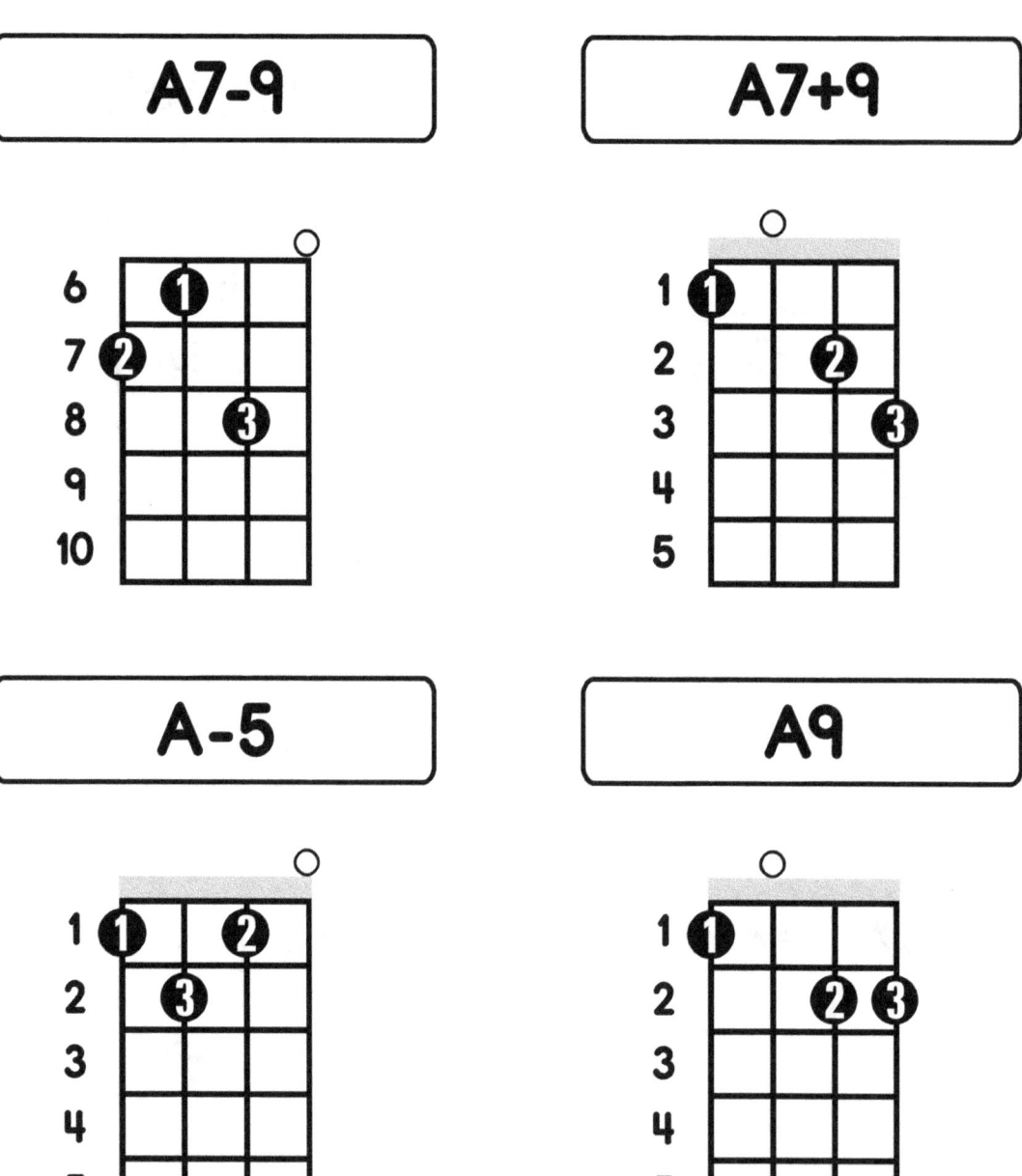

A Chords

Am9
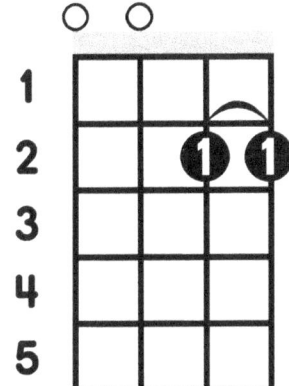

Amaj9
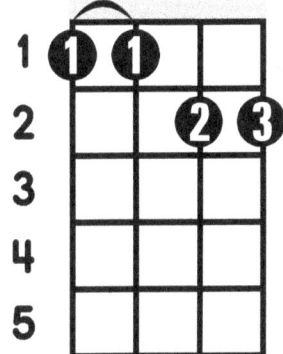

A11
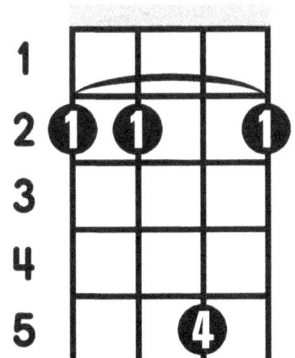

A13
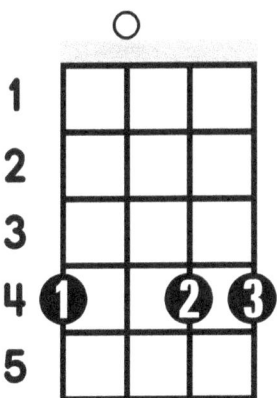

A# / B♭ Chords

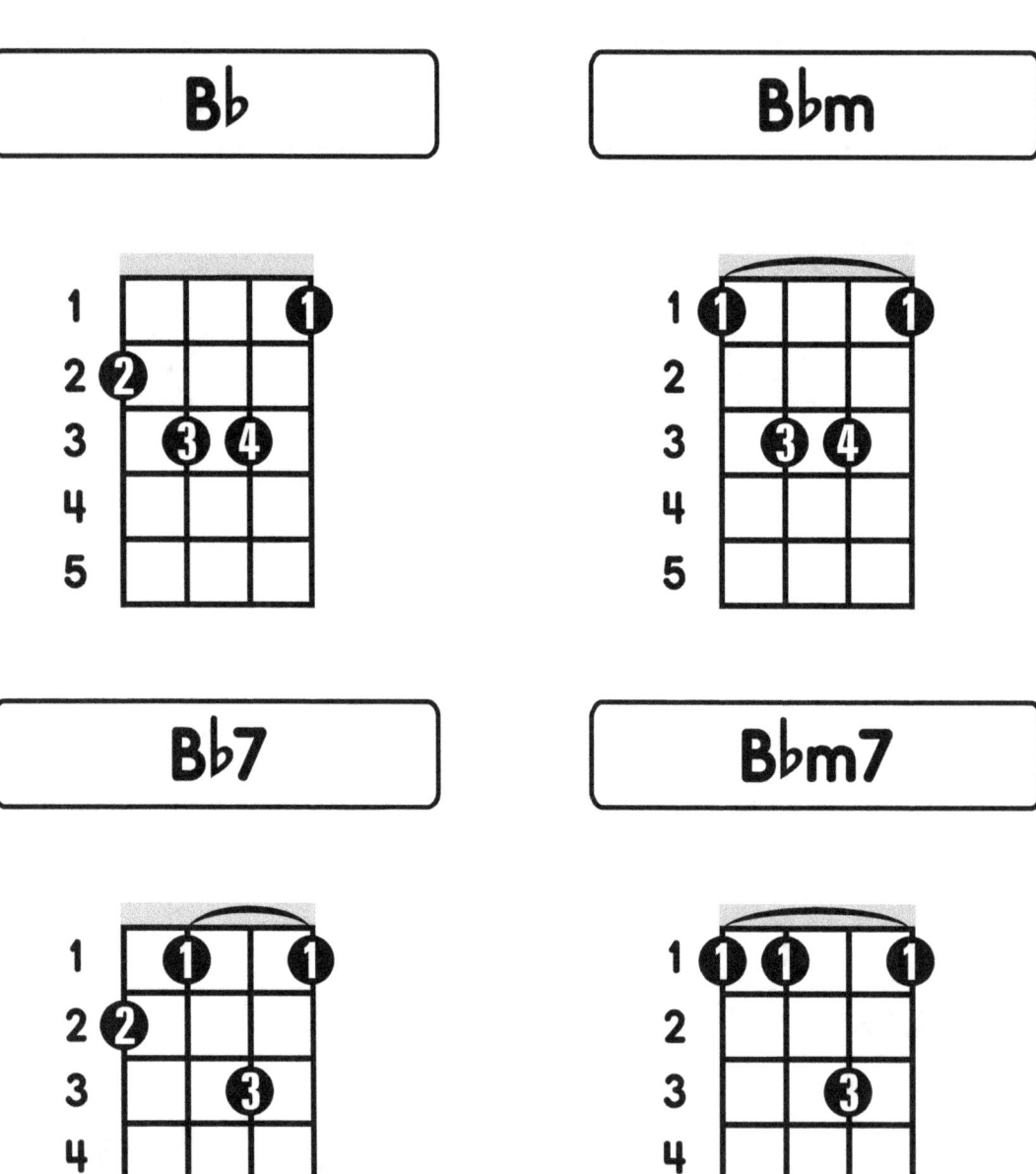

A# / B♭ Chords

B♭5

B♭6

B♭m6

B♭maj7

A# / B♭ Chords

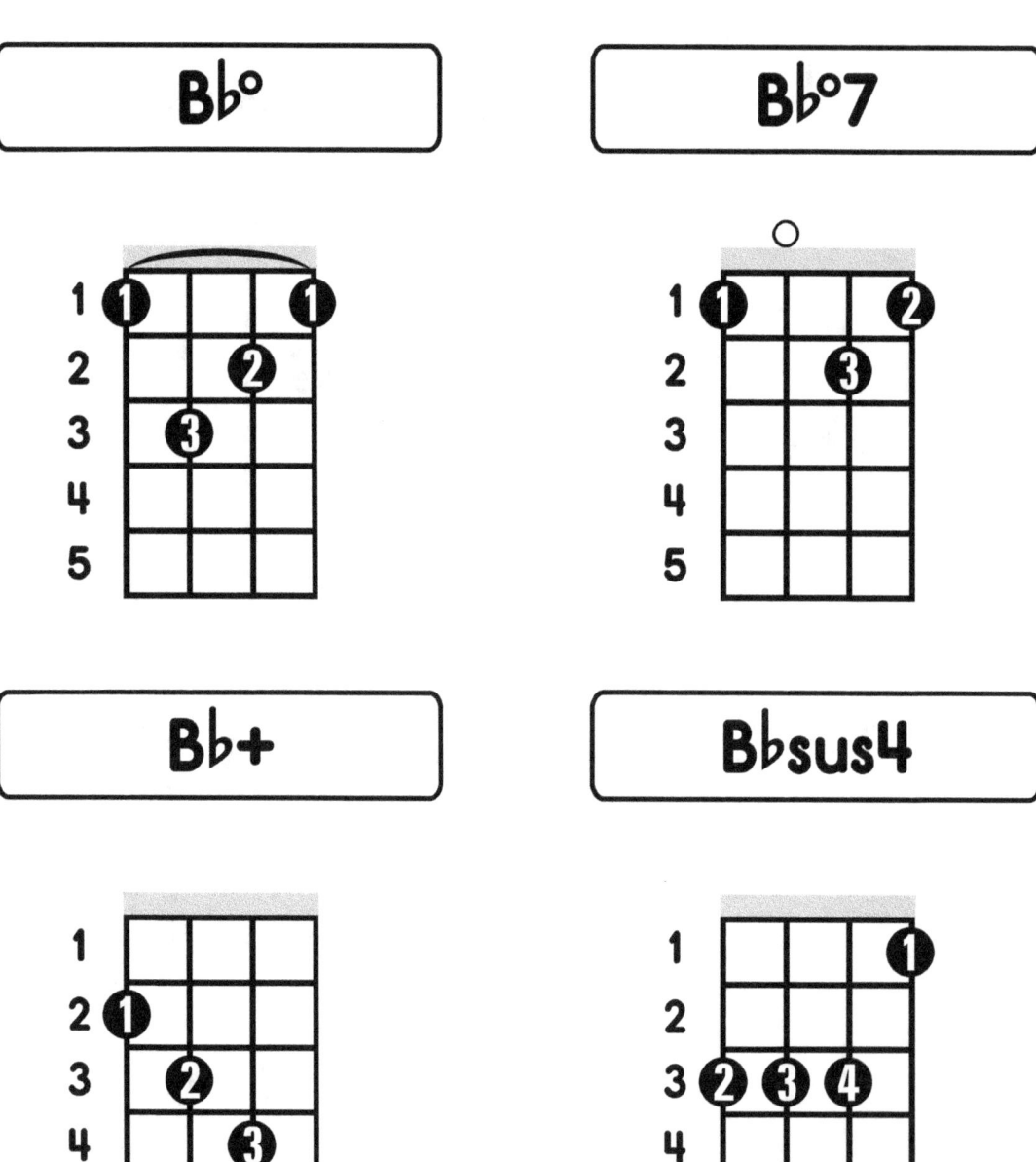

A# / Bb Chords

Bbadd9
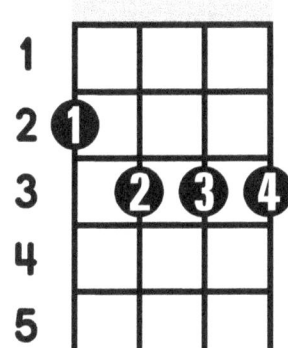

Bbmadd9
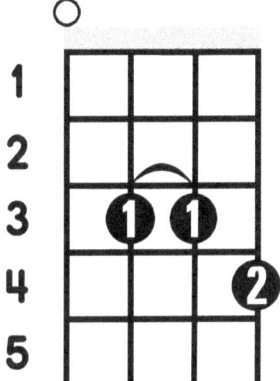

Bbm7-5
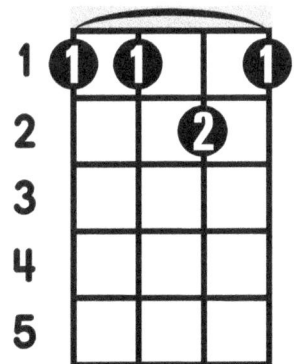

Bb7sus4
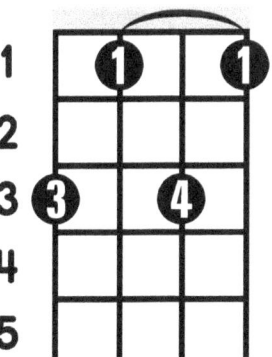

A# / B♭ Chords

B♭sus2
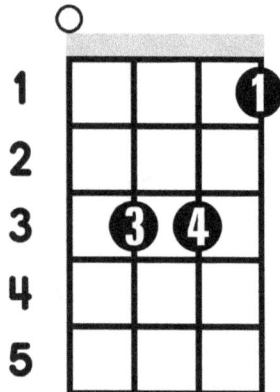

B♭m(maj7)
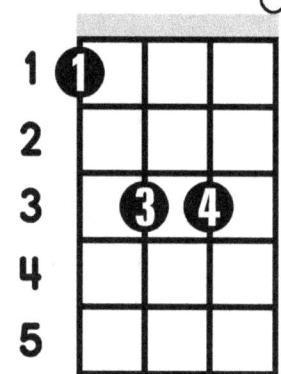

B♭7-5
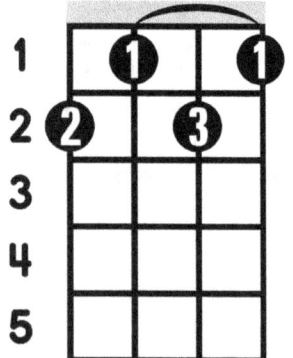

B♭7+5
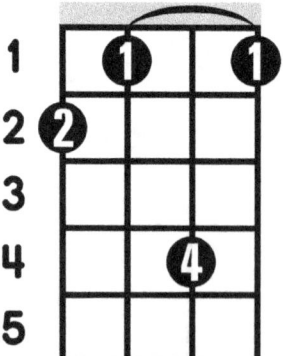

A# / Bb Chords

Bb7-9
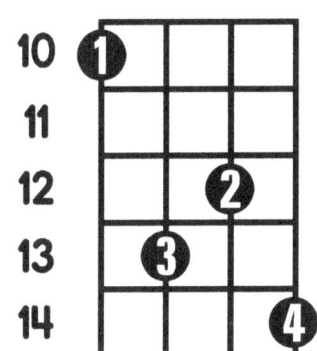

Bb7+9
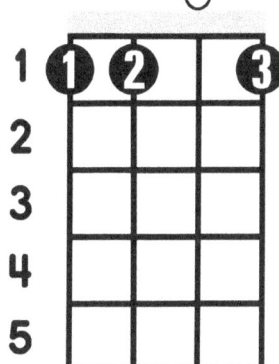

Bb-5
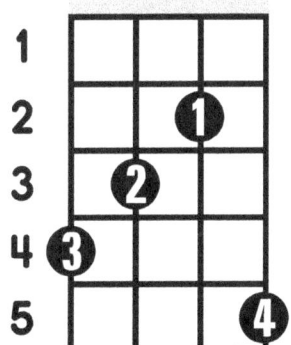

Bb9
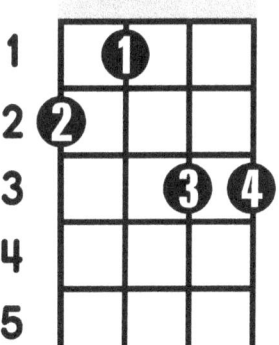

A# / B♭ Chords

B♭m9
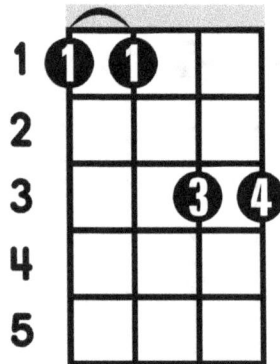

B♭maj9
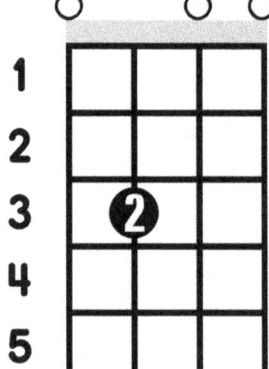

B♭11
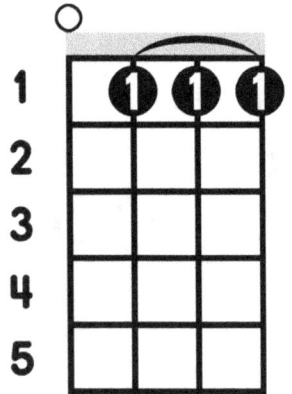

B♭13
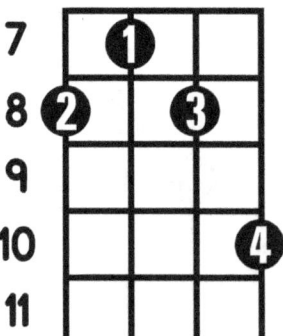

B Chords

B
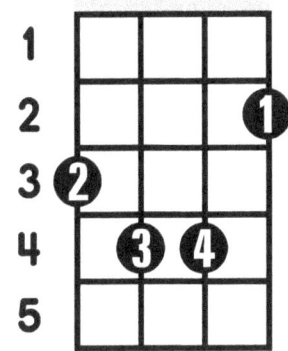

Bm
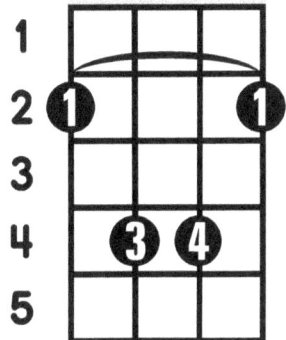

B7
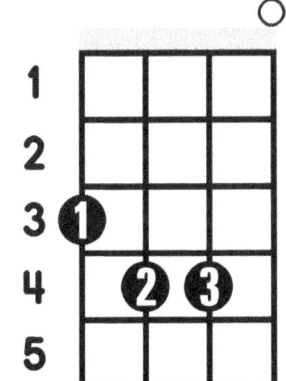

Bm7
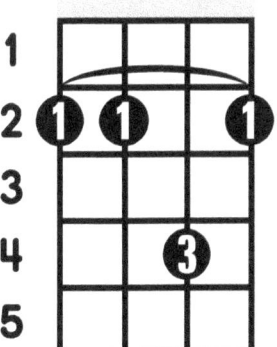

B Chords

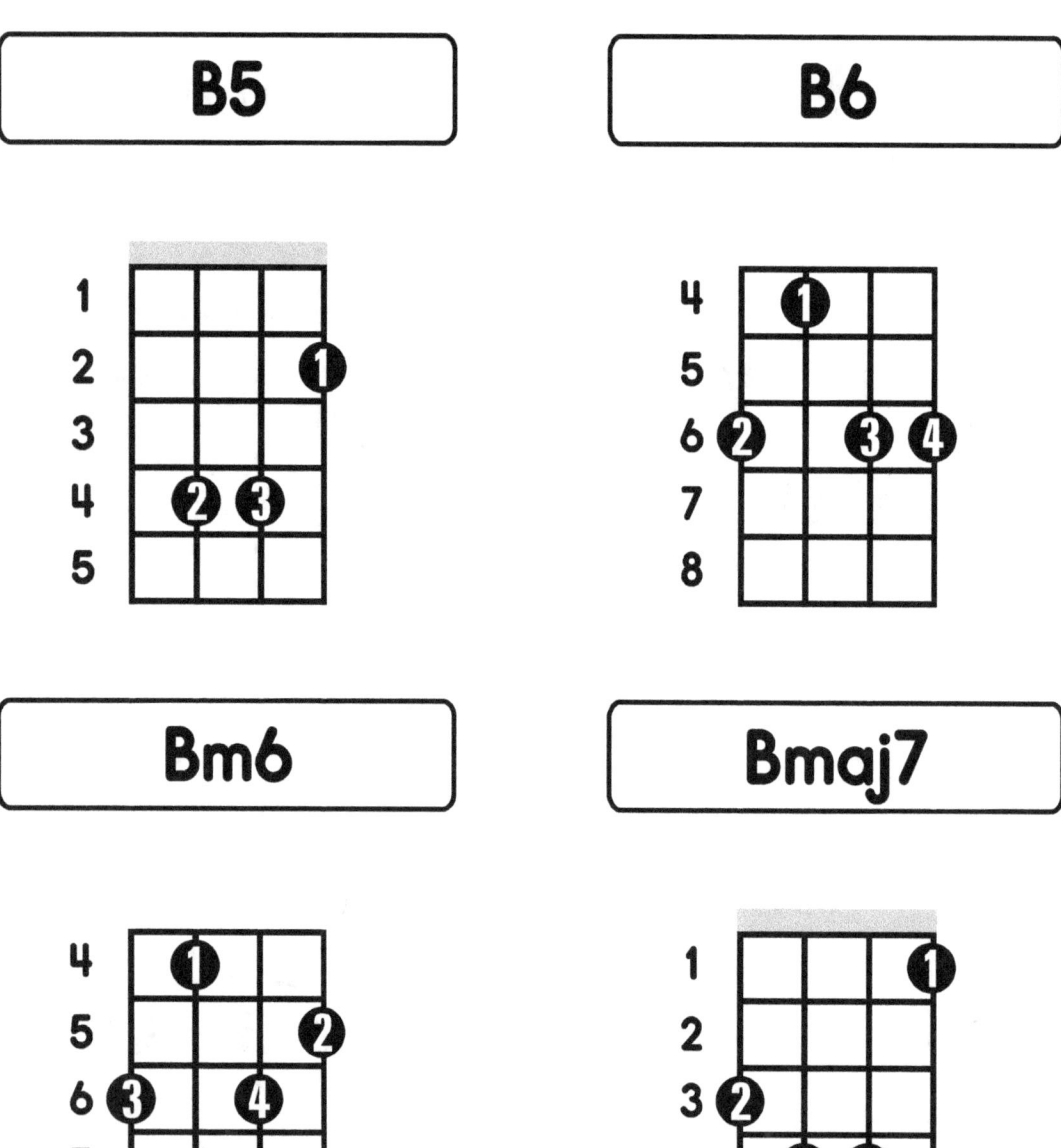

B Chords

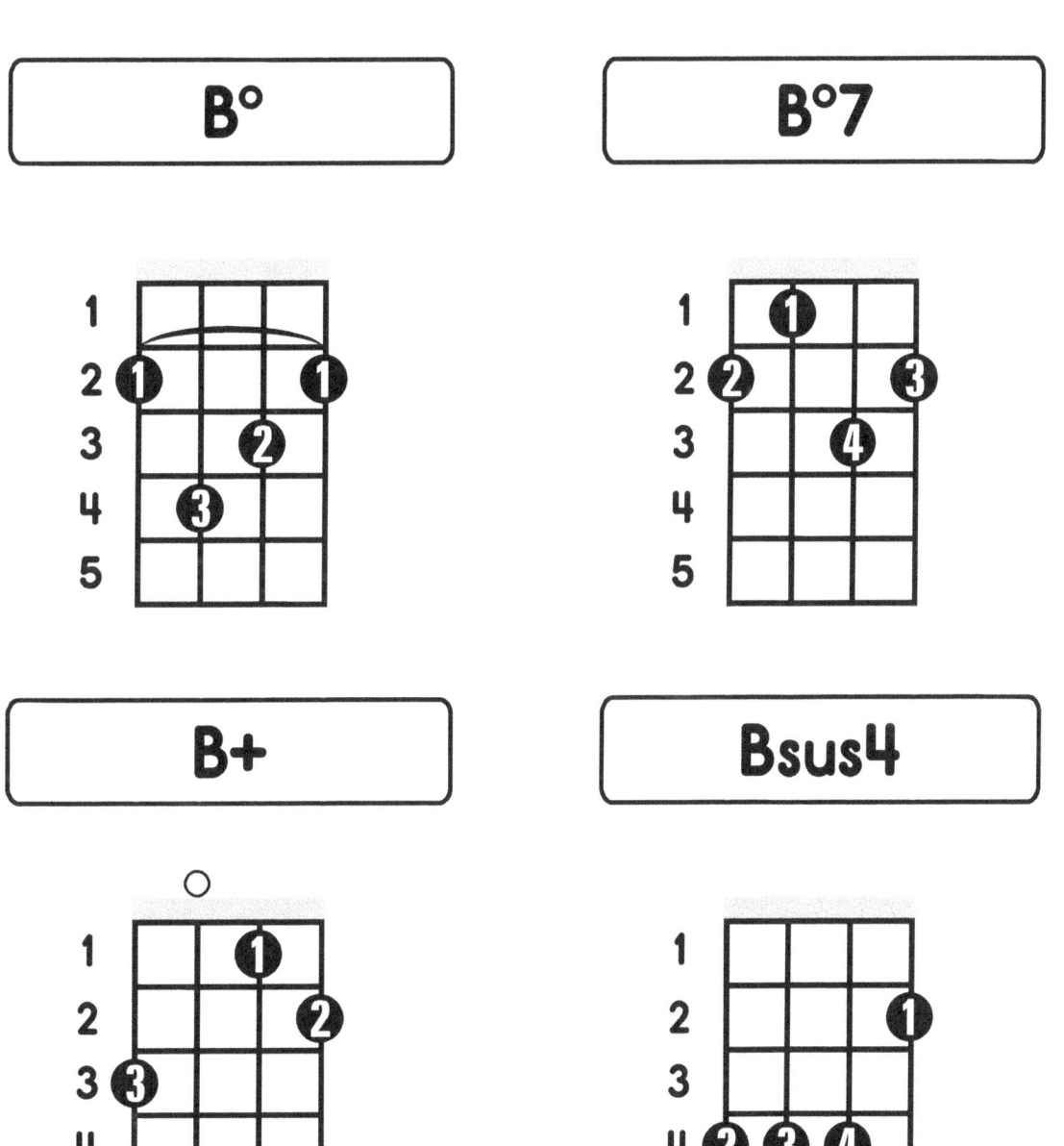

B Chords

Badd9
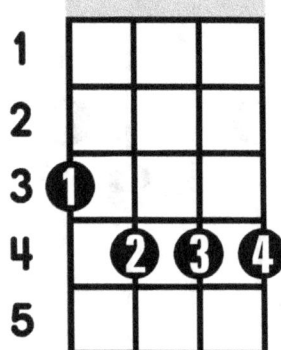

Bmadd9
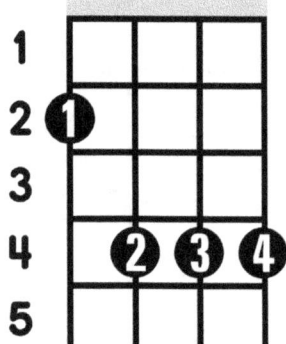

Bm7-5
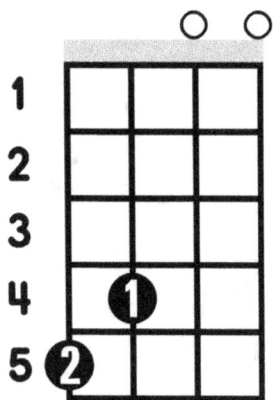

B7sus4
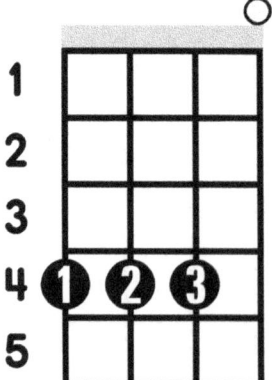

B Chords

Bsus2

Bm(maj7)

B7-5

B7+5

B Chords

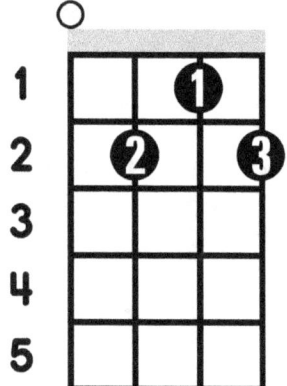

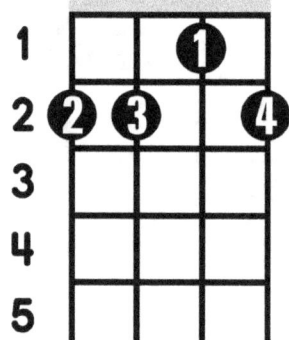

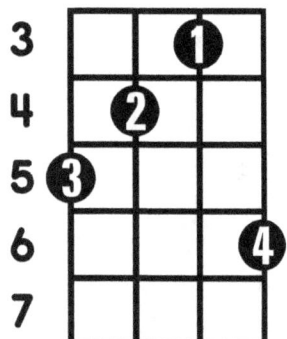
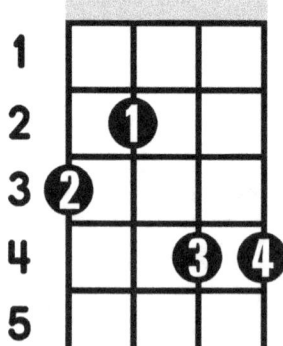

B Chords

Bm9

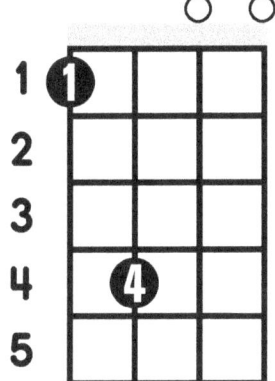

Bmaj9

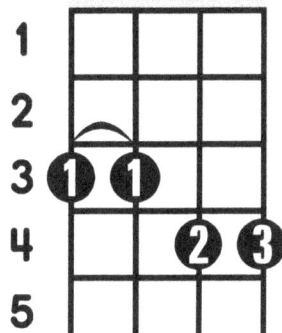

B11

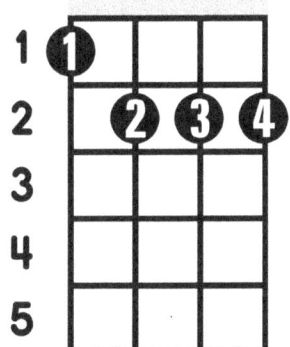

B13

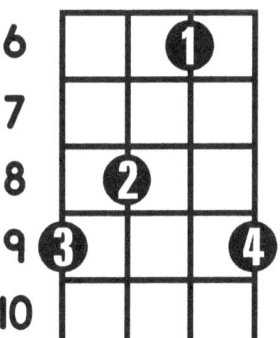

MOVEABLE CHORDS

What are moveable chords?

A moveable chord is a finger position on the tenor banjo fingerboard that stays the same even when you move that shape up and down the neck. Figure 1 shows the starting position of **E♭5**. In figure 2 the same chord shape is moved up one fret and the key is changed to **E5**. Figure 3 shows a further progression up the neck to the 3rd fret position and the chord of **F5**.

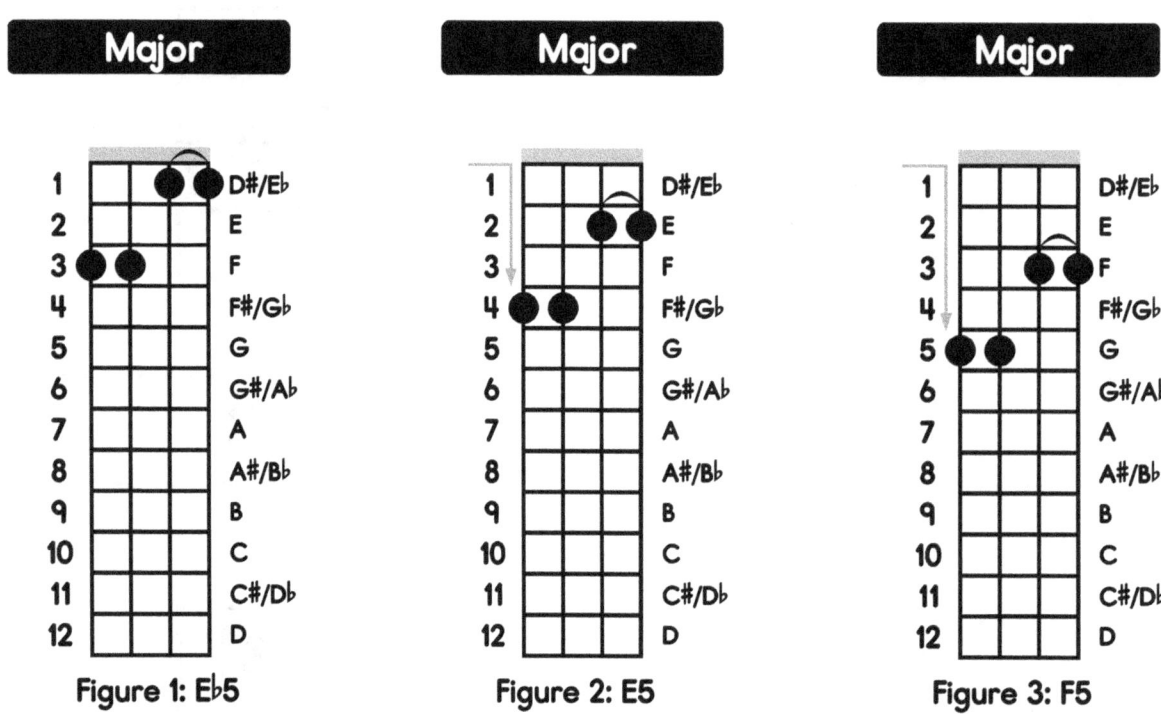

Figure 1: E♭5 Figure 2: E5 Figure 3: F5

The following pages includes a selection of 20 of the most widely used chord types for the tenor banjo, spread over 48 different examples. Using the examples given, up to 576 different chords are possible, with even more available beyond the 12th fret.

Moveable Chords

Major
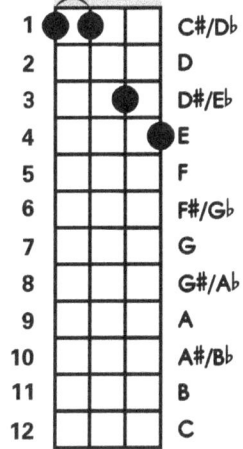

Major
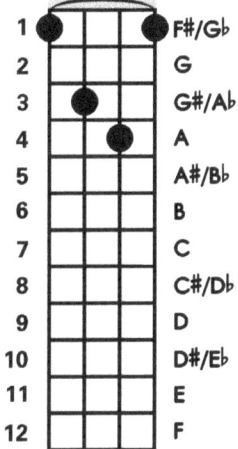

Major
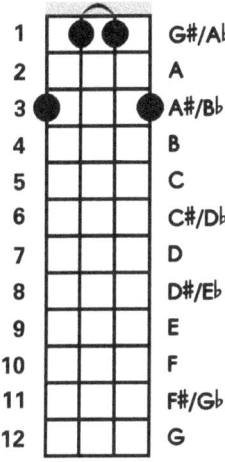

Major
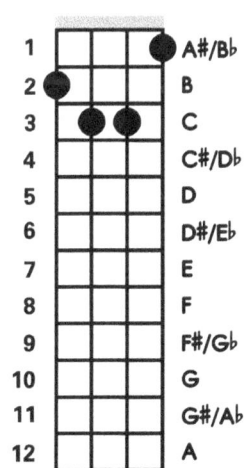

Minor
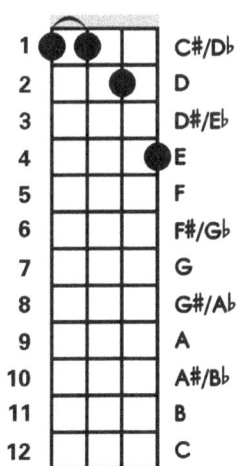

Minor
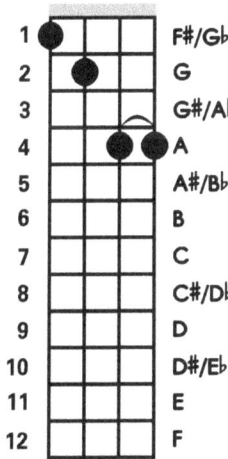

Moveable Chords

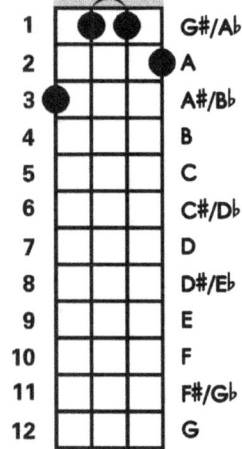
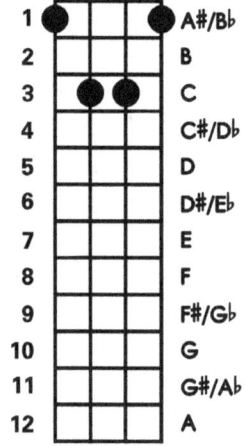
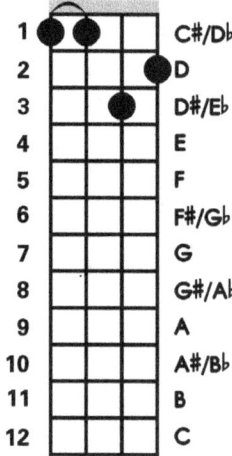
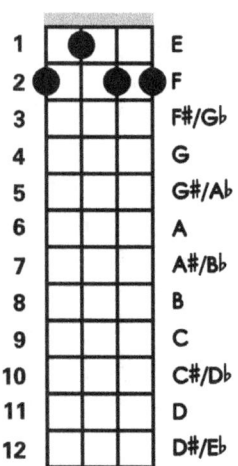
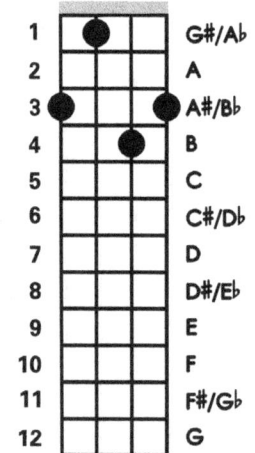
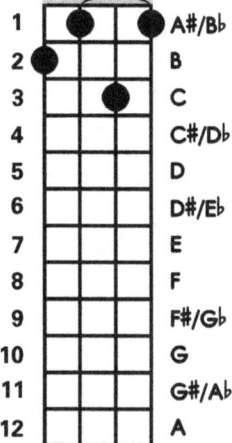

Moveable Chords

Minor Seventh
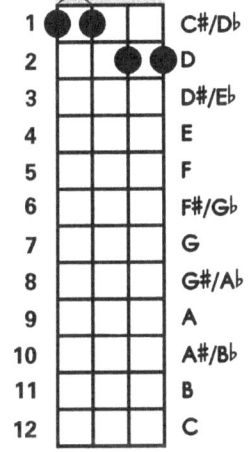

Minor Seventh
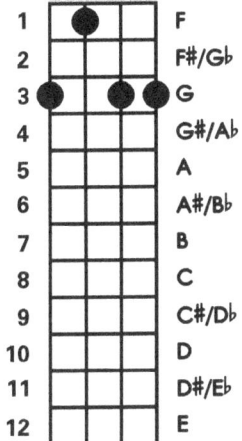

Minor Seventh
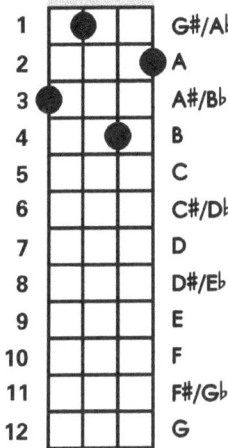

Minor Seventh
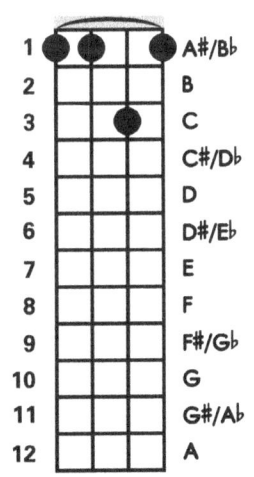

Sixth
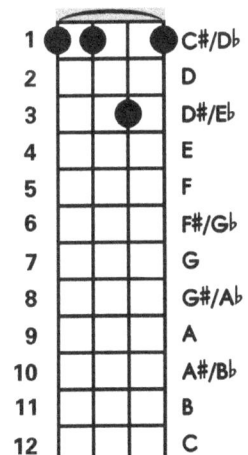

Sixth
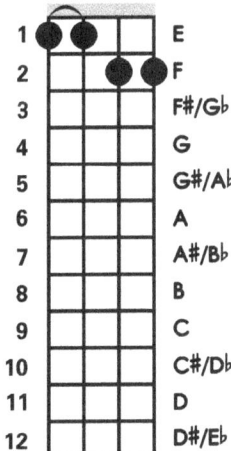

Moveable Chords

Sixth
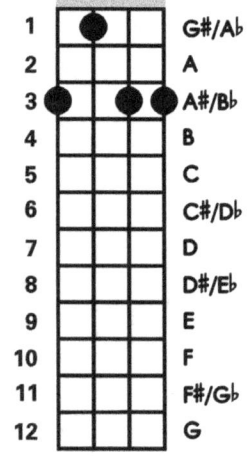

Sixth
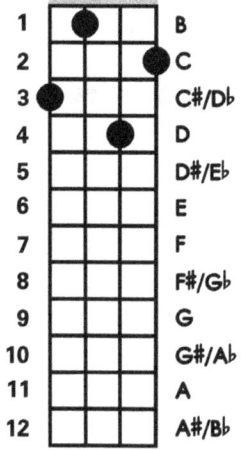

Minor Sixth
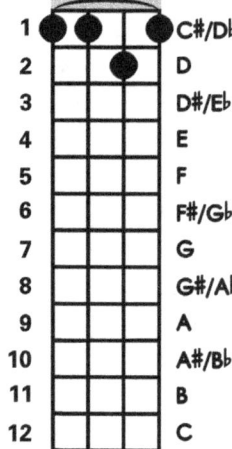

Minor Sixth
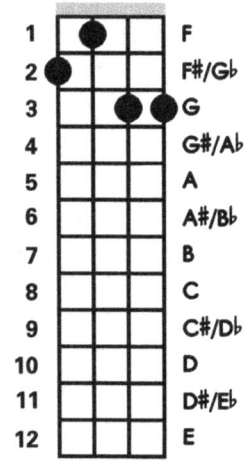

Minor Sixth
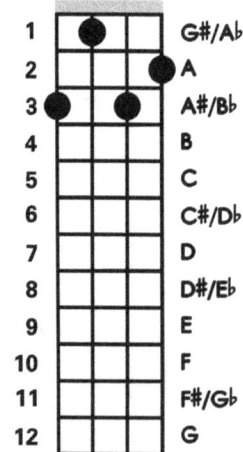

Minor Sixth
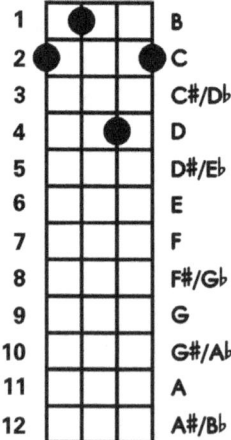

Moveable Chords

Major Seventh
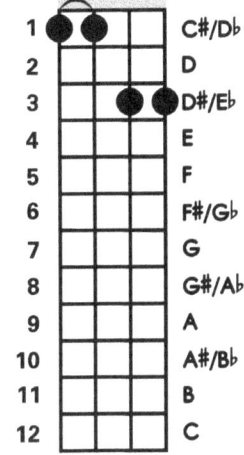

Major Seventh
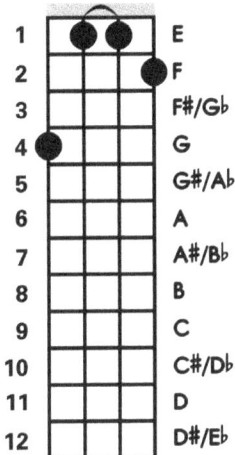

Major Seventh
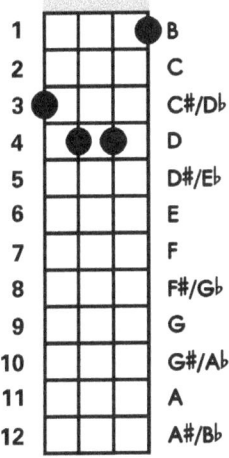

Suspended Fourth
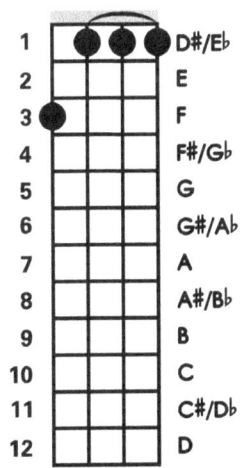

Suspended Fourth
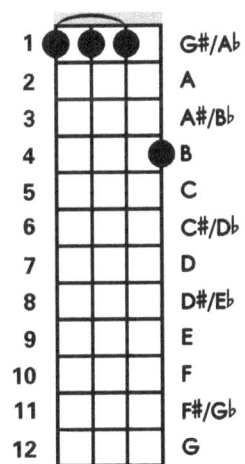

Suspended Fourth
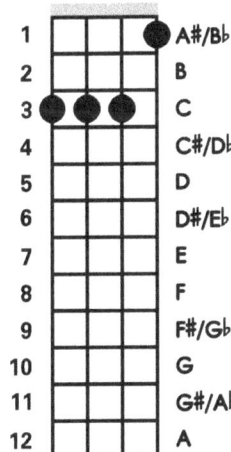

Moveable Chords

Diminished	Diminished	Diminished
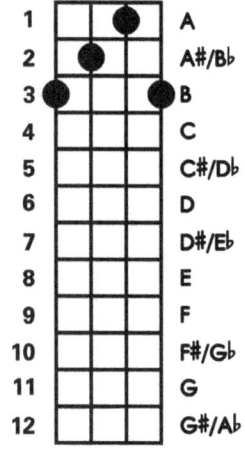	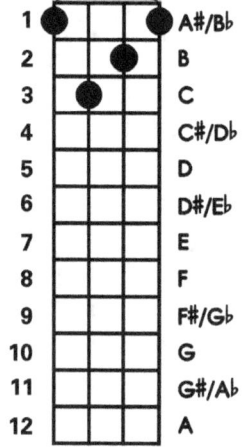	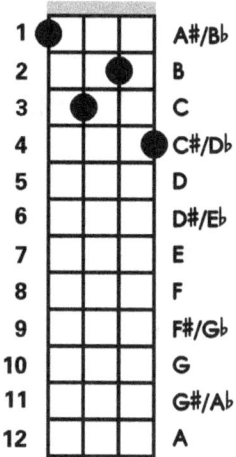

Augmented	Augmented	Augmented
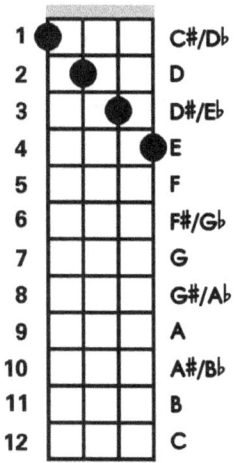	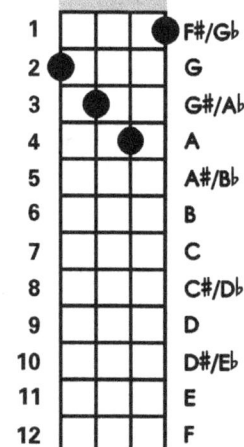	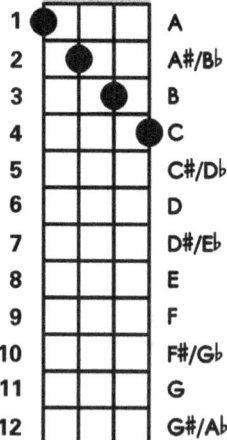

Moveable Chords

Diminished Seventh
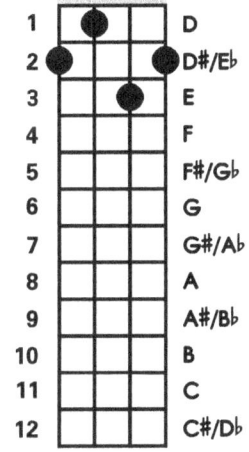

Diminished Seventh
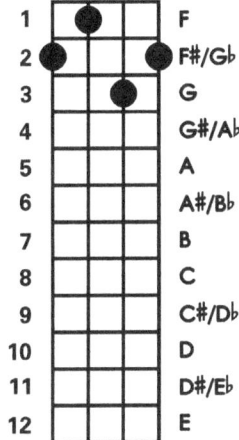

Diminished Seventh
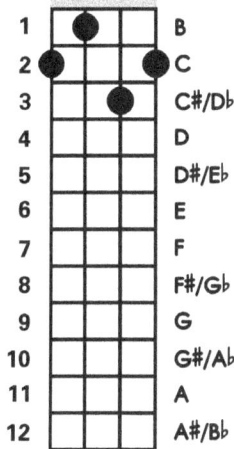

Fifth
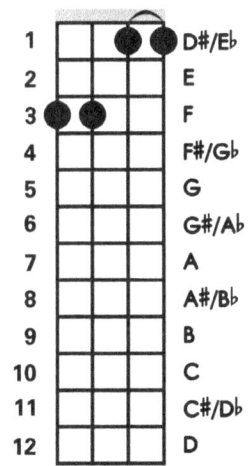

Seventh Suspended
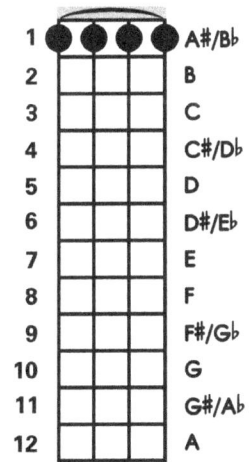

Added Ninth
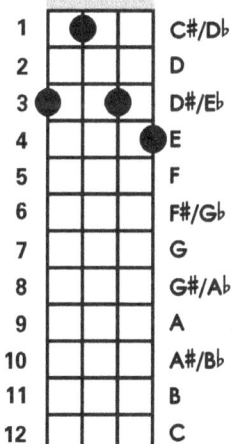

Moveable Chords

Added Ninth
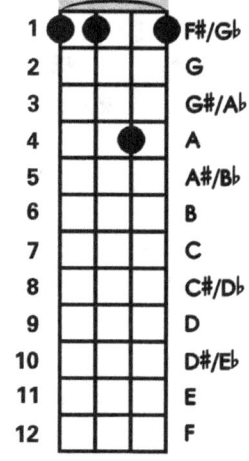

Ninth
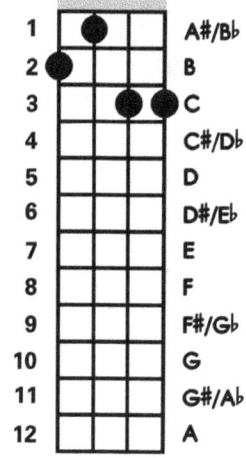

Minor Ninth
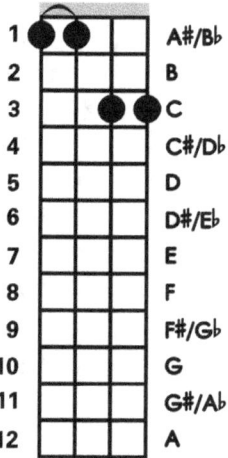

Major Ninth
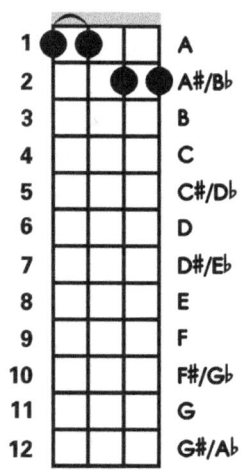

Eleventh
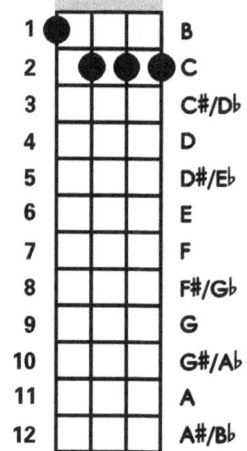

Thirteenth
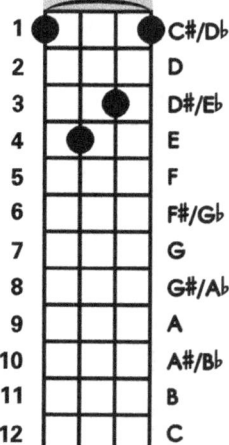

Banjo & ukulele family publications from Cabot Books

FF05 The Tenor Banjo Chord Bible: Standard Tuning (CGDA) 1,728 Chords
(ISBN 13: 978-1-906207-26-7)

FF07 The Irish Tenor Banjo Chord Bible: Standard Tuning (GDAE) 1,728 Chords
(ISBN 13: 978-1-906207-28-1)

FF18 The Plectrum Banjo Chord Bible: Standard Tuning (CGBD) 1,728 Chords
(ISBN 13: 978-1-906207-37-3)

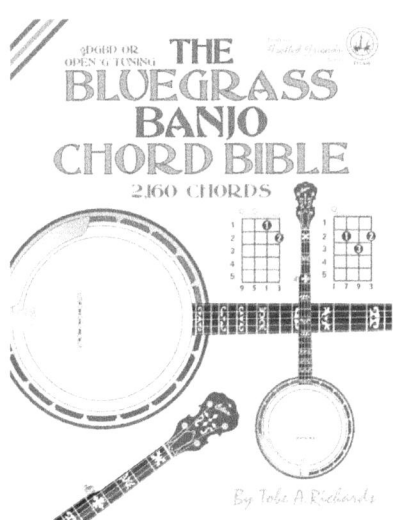

FF19 The Bluegrass Banjo Chord Bible: Open 'G' Tuning (gDGBD) 2,160 Chords
(ISBN 13: 978-1-906207-38-0)

FF08 The Ukulele Chord Bible: Standard C6 Tuning (GCEA) 2,160 Chords
(ISBN 13: 978-1-906207-29-8)

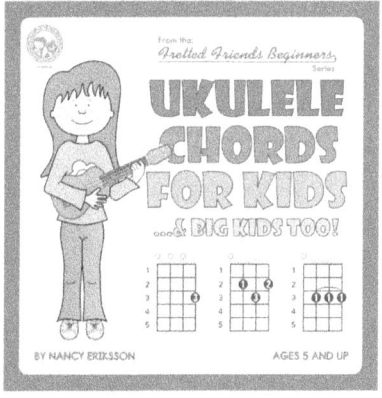

FFB08 Ukulele Chords for Kids...& Big Kids Too!
(ISBN 13: 978-1-906207-80-9)

Guitar family publications from Cabot Books

FF35 The Guitar Chord Bible: Standard Tuning 3,024 Chords
(ISBN 13: 978-1-906207-55-7)

FF36 The Left-Handed Guitar Chord Bible: Standard Tuning 3,024 Chords
(ISBN 13: 978-1-906207-56-4)

FF16 The Tenor Guitar Chord Bible: Standard & Irish Tuning 2,880 Chords
(ISBN 13: 978-1-906207-35-9)

FF31 The Baritone Guitar Chord Bible: Low B Tuning 1,728 Chords
(ISBN 13: 978-1-906207-50-2)

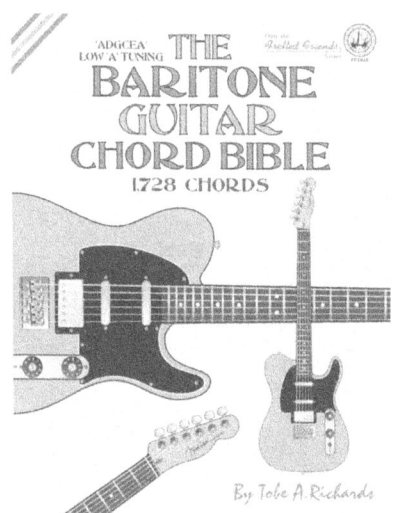

FF33 The Baritone Guitar Chord Bible: Low A Tuning 1,728 Chords
(ISBN 13: 978-1-906207-52-6)

FFB35 Guitar Chords for Kids...& Big Kids Too!
(ISBN 13: 978-1-906207-81-6)

www.ingramcontent.com/pod-product-compliance
Lightning Source LLC
Chambersburg PA
CBHW081118080526
44587CB00021B/3643